EXERCISES
for

THE
EVERYDAY
WRITER

A Brief Reference

Lex Runciman
LINFIELD COLLEGE

Francine Weinberg

ST. MARTIN'S PRESS
New York

Manufactured in the United States of America.

1 0 9 8 7
f e d c b a

For information, write:
St. Martin's Press, Inc.
175 Fifth Avenue
New York, NY 10010

ISBN 0-312-14827-5

Contents

SENTENCE GRAMMAR   20

WORDS / GLOSSARY   65

PUNCTUATION / MECHANICS   80

FOR MULTILINGUAL WRITERS   106

ANSWERS TO THE EVEN-NUMBERED EXERCISES

Preface

Exercises for The Everyday Writer is a resource for teachers and students. Its exercises consist of sentences and paragraphs needing revision, most of them designed so that students can edit directly on the pages of this book.

The exercise sets are numbered to correspond to chapters in *The Everyday Writer*. Students can quickly locate help by following the cross-references in each exercise's instructions to specific pages in *The Everyday Writer*.

To help students check their own progress as they work, answers to the even-numbered exercise items appear in the back of this book. Exercises with many possible answers—those asking students to imitate a sentence or revise a paragraph, for example—are not answered here. Answers to the odd-numbered exercises are given in the instructor's answer key only.

If you have adopted *The Everyday Writer* as a text, you are welcome to photocopy any of these exercises to use for homework assignments, for classroom activities, for quizzes. The book is also available for student purchase.

Frequently Asked Questions

Recognizing and eliminating the twenty most common errors

Revise each of the following numbered items to eliminate one of the twenty most common sentence-level errors written by first-year students. (See *The Everyday Writer*, pp. 1–24.) Example:

> **Learning another language is not a matter of genes; ̶i̶t̶s̶ a matter of hard work.**
>
> (correction above: *it's*)

1. The Beast, which is one of the biggest roller coasters, has a thunderous ride of steep hills and turns. As you race down the first and biggest hill your coaster is engulfed by a tunnel at the end of the hill.

2. Once you find where other surfers are, you can set up your camp. This entails claiming your own territory. You do this by laying out your over-sized beach towel and by turning your radio on loud enough to mark your domain without disturbing anyone else. This should help you blend in with the locals.

3. I was gaining speed and feeling really good but when I looked back he wasn't there. I panicked. I saw him and my parents down at the other end of the street and forgot to look forward. When I finally did turn forward, I saw that I was rapidly closing in on my neighbor's car.

4. Assateague is perfect for those who want to simply lay out in the sun, go swimming, and walk along the coast. But for those who crave a little more excitement, Ocean City is just a few minutes away by car.

5. The knights with armor and horses beautifully decorated participate in battles of jousting, target shooting with spears, archery, and duels of strategy and strength using swords and shields. During the evening, there is a break from the fighting, and a beautiful ceremony of marriage is acted out.

6. I decided to begin searching for an outfit while the rollers in my hair cooled. I began throwing everything out of my closet. Nothing fits my mood, and not one thing caught my eyes as they fell on the bed. I had no idea what I was even looking for since I didn't know where I was going.

7. You should also think about how far you want to walk to class from your apartment. You may want to live in an apartment that is a shorter walking distance to campus, especially if it is important to you to be independent from public transportation.

8. Chips and sauces are not the only thing that you get free refills on, you also get free refills on all nonalcoholic beverages, such as soda and tea. The servers are very good about getting you more of both things when you need refills, usually you do not even have to ask.

9. What I'm trying to get at is that because of this persons immaturity, many people have suffered. This persons lack of responsibility has turned peoples lives upside down.

10. The good thing about its location is that it is right off the main highway, very easy to spot. There are also plenty of road signs pointing you in the right direction of the park. And if you got extremely lost, pulling off and asking would be the easiest way to get on track.

11. After deciding to begin your college career, many students are then faced with the predicament of where to live. This matter is not such a problem for students from out of town, but it is if you live in the same city or area in which you chose a school.

12. When I got to half court, the guy that was playing center on my team stood between the defensive player and me. As I dribbled around the center, he stopped the defensive player. Not by using his hands but by his big body.

13. I thought about all the work we had done this quarter in English. I had not done well on my spelling tests even when I had cheated on them. I did my reading assignments with other people so I never answered the question by myself completely.

14. Their hands are folded, and it seems as though they are mumbling to themselves. They try to get the person's attention but never does what they planned to do.

15. I was driving along behind an older Volkswagen Jetta, following closely, but not close enough that I couldn't see everything that was going on around me. My eyes were watching the brake lights the curbs the sidewalks, and the car in front of me.

16. On the other hand, what if you don't care for your partner—or even worse—they don't care for you? You know now that it is still okay to separate without the problem of obtaining a divorce. Many divorces that take place within the first few years of marriage might be avoided if the couple had lived together before marrying.

17. There is also a stand-up roller coaster called, King Kobra, which goes upside down in the first loop, with plenty of tossing and turning. As I said previously, King's Island also keeps the people with weaker stomachs in mind; throughout the park, there are rides that are a little slower-paced.

18. I felt someone's hand shaking my shoulder. I lifted my head up to see my best friend, Stephanie, looking down at me. "That must have been some dream. Come on the bell rang class is over."

19. Trying to keep parents happy is a constant effort made by kids to keep in good standing with mom and dad. After all, it is they who will support us until we are capable of living on our own with things like money, food, and clothes.

20. You cannot just decide to have a party and have it the same day. You have to prepare for it. All the things that you do before, during, and after the party determine it's success. The better you prepare for it, the better time everyone will have.

Sentence Style

9.1 Matching subjects and predicates

Revise each of the following sentences in two ways to make its structures consistent in grammar and meaning. (See *The Everyday Writer,* p. 61.) Example:

> Because
> ~~The fact that~~ our room was cold, we put a heater between our beds.
>   ^   ^
>
> The fact that our room was cold led us to put a heater between our beds.

1. My interest in a political career would satisfy my desire for public service.

2. To determine your rank, your supervisor should be consulted.

3. The reason air-pollution standards should not be relaxed is because many people would suffer.

4. By not prosecuting white-collar crime as vigorously as violent crime encourages white-collar criminals to think they can ignore the law.

5. Herman Melville's stature is unchallenged, including not only *Moby Dick* but also many legendary short stories.

6. A stroke is when there is a shortage of blood to the brain.

7. Hawthorne's short stories are experiences drawn from his own life.

8. When Oedipus suddenly realizes he has killed his father and married his mother causes a "shock of recognition."

9. One controversial element of the curriculum has been colleges with a required course in Western culture.

10. The European discovery of Australia became a penal colony for Britain.

9.2 Making comparisons complete, consistent, and clear

Revise each of the following sentences to eliminate any inappropriate elliptical constructions; to make comparisons complete, logically consistent, and clear; and to supply any other omitted words that are necessary for meaning. (See *The Everyday Writer*, p. 63.) Example:

is
Most of the candidates are bright, and one brilliant.
^

1. My new stepmother makes my father happier.

2. Argentina and Peru were colonized by Spain, and Brazil by Portugal.

3. She argued that children are even more important for men than women.

4. Was the dictatorship in Iraq any worse than many other countries?

5. The personalities of marijuana smokers are different from nonsmokers.

6. Tim decided to take a nap, Michael decided to study for his chemistry test, and Susan to take a book back to the library.

7. The car's exterior is blue, but the seats black vinyl.

8. Cats eat fish, and cats even eat liver but rarely a steak.

9. The house is Victorian, its windows enormous.

10. As time went on, the baby became less animated and interested.

9.3 Revising for consistency and completeness

Revise this paragraph so that all sentences are grammatically and logically consistent and complete. (See *The Everyday Writer*, pp. 61–63.)

The reason I believe the United States should have a military draft is because a draft would make us better citizens. By requiring the same sacrifice from every young person would make everyone feel part a common effort. In addition, a draft is fairer. When an army is made up of volunteers come mostly from the poor and minority groups. During the Persian Gulf War, news reports showed blacks were overrepresented among the troops, largely because their economic options were more limited than young whites and the military thus more attractive as a career. I also feel that women should be subject to the draft. A quality that the military needs is soldiers who are dedicated, and women soldiers have shown that they are more dedicated to their jobs than men. The requirements of a modern army also need skills that more women possess. Equality is when both sexes have equal responsibilities as well as equal opportunity.

10.1 Combining sentences with coordination

Using the principles of coordination to signal equal importance or to create special emphasis, combine and revise the following twelve short sentences into several longer and more effective ones. Add or delete words as necessary. (See *The Everyday Writer,* pp. 64–69.)

The bull-riding arena was fairly crowded.
The crowd made no impression on me.
I had made a decision.
It was now time to prove myself.
I was scared.
I walked to the entry window.
I laid my money on the counter.
The clerk held up a Stetson hat filled with slips of paper.
I reached in.
I picked one.
The slip held the number of the bull I was to ride.
I headed toward the stock corral.

10.2 Writing sentences with subordination

Combine each of the following sets of sentences into one sentence that uses subordination to signal the relationships among ideas. Add or delete words as necessary. (See *The Everyday Writer*, pp. 66–69.) Example:

> **I was looking over my books.**
> **I noticed that *Burr* was missing.**
> **This book is a favorite of my roommate's.**

> While I was looking over my books, I noticed that *Burr*, one of my roommate's favorite books, was missing.

1. I walked into the shelter.

   Men, women, and children were slumped against the wall.

   Shopping carts containing families' belongings lay on their sides.

2. Barbra Streisand announced her first concert tour in years.

   Ticket sales were advertised.

   Fans lined up as many as forty-eight hours in advance.

3. We had dug a seventy-foot ditch.

   My boss would pour gravel into the ditch.

   I would level the gravel with a shovel.

4. *Working* was written by Studs Terkel.

   It is an important book.

   It examines the situation of the American worker.

5. The scenery there is beautiful.

   The mountains have caps of snow.

   The lakes are deep and full of fish.

   The pastures are green.

   It is an ideal spot to spend spring break.

10.3 Using coordination and subordination

Revise the following paragraph, using coordination and subordination where appropriate to clarify the relationships between ideas. (See *The Everyday Writer*, pp. 64–69.)

I stayed with my friend Louise. She owns a huge, mangy wolf. It is actually a seven-eighths wolf cross. The poor creature is allergic to everything. It looks like a shabby, moth-eaten exhibit of a stuffed wolf in a third-rate museum. Louise and Bill feed it rice and raw potatoes. It slavers all over everything. It never goes out of the house. It sleeps on the beds. They are covered with animal hair. It makes no sounds. It just looks at you with those sunken, wild eyes. It is not dangerous or ferocious. It is just completely miserable. This animal should never have been born. It's trying to tell you that with every twitch.

11.1 Creating parallel words or phrases

Complete the following sentences, using parallel words or phrases in each case. (See *The Everyday Writer*, pp. 69–72.) Example:

The wise politician _promises the possible_ , _effects the unavoidable_ ,

and _accepts the inevitable_ .

1. Before we depart, we must _____ , _____ , and

   _____ .

2. My favorite pastimes include _____ , _____ ,

   and _____ .

3. We must either _____ or _____ .

4. I want not only _____ but also _____ .

5. Graduates find that the job market _____,

_____ , and _____ .

6. _____ , _____ , and _____ are

activities my grandparents enjoy.

7. By the terms of the treaty, the nations agreed _____ and

_____ .

8. I told my younger sister _____ and _____ .

9. I left the book _____ , _____ , or

_____ .

10. My motto is _____ , _____ , and

_____ .

11.2   Revising sentences for parallelism

Revise the following sentences to eliminate any errors in parallel
structure. (See *The Everyday Writer*, pp. 69–72.) Example:

>   *collecting*
> **I enjoy skiing, playing the piano, and ~~I collect~~ movie posters.**
>   ^

1. I remember entering the stark canyon in North Dakota, searching the
   rubble by day, sleeping in a tent by night, and at last discovered
   dinosaur bones.

2. I will always remember how the girls dressed in green plaid skirts and
   the boys wearing green plaid ties.

3. It was a question of either reducing their staff, or they had to somehow
   find new customers for their baked potatoes.

4. To need a new pair of shoes and not being able to afford a pair is sad.

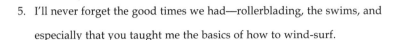
5. I'll never forget the good times we had—rollerblading, the swims, and especially that you taught me the basics of how to wind-surf.

6. Too many students come to college only for fun, to find a husband or wife, or in order to put off having to go to work.

7. There are two types of wallflowers: the male wallflower is known as the nerd, and the female, who is known as the skeeve.

8. Her job was to show new products, help with sales, and an opportunity to be part of advertising.

9. The Greek system not only provides the individual with a circle of friends but also it contributes to the development of leadership skills.

10. Stress can result in low self-esteem, total frustration, being unable to sleep, nervous breakdown, or eventually in suicide.

11.3 Revising for parallelism and supplying necessary words

Revise the following paragraph to maintain parallelism and to supply all words necessary for clarity, grammar, and idiom in parallel structures. (See *The Everyday Writer,* pp. 69–72.)

Growing up in a large city provides a very different experience from a suburban childhood. Suburban children undoubtedly enjoy many advantages over those who live in a city, including lawns to play ball on, trees for climbing, and often the schools are better. However, in recent years many people raised in the suburbs but who moved to large cities as young adults are deciding to bring up their own children in an urban setting. Their reasons for doing so include what they consider the cultural advantages of the city, the feeling that they will be able to spend more time with their children if they do not have to commute so far to work, and also they want to expose the children to a greater diversity of social and economic groups than most suburbs offer. Just as their own parents left the city for the space and calm of suburbia, so crowds and excitement are why today's parents are returning to it. Wherever they bring up their children, though, parents have never nor will they ever find utopia.

12.1   Revising for verb tense and mood

Revise any of the following sentences in which you find unnecessary shifts in verb tense or in mood. (See *The Everyday Writer,* p. 73.) Examples:

> $\overset{\text{does}}{}$
> The newspaper covers campus events, but it ~~did~~ not appeal to students.
>
> Walk over to the field house, and then ~~you should~~ get in line.
> $\wedge$

1. The day is hot, stifling, and typical of July, a day when no one willingly ventured out onto the burning asphalt.

2. Then, suddenly, the big day arrives. The children were still a bit sleepy, for their anticipation had kept them awake.

3. Place a test strip on the subject area; you should expose the test strip to light and develop it for two and a half minutes.

4. I think it is better that Grandfather die painlessly, bravely, and with dignity than that he continues to live in terrible physical pain.

5. The importance of music to society is evident throughout the entire magazine. A good example was the first advertisement.

6. A cloud of snow powder rose as skis and poles fly in every direction.

7. Whether women be homemakers or are executives, they deserve respect.

8. The coroner asked that we be quiet and that we should be attentive.

9. The jogging mania of the 1970s gave way to the aerobics craze of the 1980s, which in turn gives way to the Stairmaster fad of the 1990s.

10. Say no to drugs, and you should consider alcohol a drug, too!

12.2 Eliminating shifts in voice and point of view

Revise each of the following sentences to eliminate an unnecessary shift in voice or point of view. (See *The Everyday Writer,* p. 74.) Examples:

    she prefers
Although she enjoys rock music, jazz. is preferred by her.
                              ^   ^

                                                  they
Zoo patrons should be sure to visit the aviary, and you shouldn't miss
                                                     ^
the elephant house.

1. My grandmother was wise, but her wisdom was usually ignored by the family.

2. The roses were gathered by Lionel, and then he arranged them.

3. Suddenly we heard an explosion of wings off to our right, and you could see a hundred or more ducks lifting off from the water.

4. If one visits the local art museum, you will find on display recent prints by Greg Pfarr.

5. When someone says "roommate" to a high school senior bound for college, thoughts of no privacy and potential fights are conjured up.

6. The first thing that is seen as we start down the slope is a green banner.

7. I liked the sense of individualism, the crowd yelling for you, and the feeling that I was in command.

8. Sea anemones thrive in coastal tide pools, but it cannot survive outside the water for very long.

9. The physician moves the knee around to observe the connections of the cartilage and ligaments, and a fluid is injected into the joint.

10. Tourists should be aware that road crews are busy on Highway 34, and a driver should expect some delay at the Oglesby Bridge construction site.

12.3 Eliminating shifts between direct and indirect discourse

To eliminate the shifts between direct and indirect discourse in the following sentences, put the direct discourse into indirect form. (See *The Everyday Writer,* p. 74.) Example:

              states   his
Steven Pinker ~~stated~~ that ~~my~~ book is meant for people who use
            ^   ^
language and respect it.

1. Loren Eiseley feels an urge to join the birds in their soundless flight, but in the end he knows that he cannot, and "I was, after all, only a man."

2. According to the article, the ozone layer is rapidly dwindling, and "we are endangering the lives of future generations."

3. The instructor told us, "Please read the next two stories before the next class" and that she might give us a quiz on them.

4. Oscar Wilde writes that books cannot be divided into moral and immoral categories, and "books are either well-written or badly written."

5. Richard Rodriguez acknowledges that intimacy was not created by a language; "it is created by intimates."

12.4 Eliminating shifts in tone and diction

Revise each of the following sentences to eliminate shifts in tone and diction. (See *The Everyday Writer*, p. 75.) Example:

How do I
Excuse me. ~~In which direction should I proceed to~~ get to the mall?
⌃

1. The totally unexpected message that my mother was suffering from an aneurysm really bummed me out.

2. George Washington was a leader of men; he even led a bunch of his people across the Potomac and into a bunch of fights with the British.

3. The Guggenheim exhibit of African works of art, often misunderstood and undervalued by Western art historians, is a heck of a show.

4. You have no permission to drive over my land willy-nilly with total impunity.

5. Most commuters keep to a predictable schedule, hopping a bus or train to the 'burbs at the same time each night.

13.1 Emphasizing main ideas

Revise each of the following sentences to highlight what you take to be the main or most important ideas. (See *The Everyday Writer*, pp. 76–77.) Example:

Theories about dinosaurs run the gamut—simple lizards, fully

adapted warmblooded creatures/. hybrids of coldblooded capabilities/,

1. All medical papers, whether initial investigation, presentation of final statistics, or reports on work in progress, must undergo rigorous scrutiny.

2. Coast Guard personnel conduct boating safety classes, sometimes must risk their own lives to save others, and monitor emergency radio channels.

3. Also notable is the image of chrysanthemums throughout the story.

4. John Kennedy became president after being elected to Congress and after distinguished service as a PT boat commander during World War II.

5. Steffi Graff went on to win the U.S. Open in 1996, despite the preceding media circus.

6. After he blew a tire out, Al Unser sped across the finish line, thanks to his trusty pit crew and his ability to control the car in a tailspin.

7. The presence of the American Indian in these movies always conjures up destructive stereotypes of bloodthirsty war parties, horse thieves, and drunkenness.

8. The case baffled inspectors—even though they found the killer eventually—because of the bizarre nature of the clues and the fact that no one ever heard a thing.

9. Victorian women were warned that if they smoked, they would become sterile, grow a mustache, die young, or contract tuberculosis.

10. Margaret was in medical school for over six years, she finally graduated last month, and she had spent three years deciding whether medicine was right for her.

14.1 Eliminating unnecessary words and phrases

Make each of the following sentences clear and concise by eliminating unnecessary words and phrases. (See *The Everyday Writer,* pp. 78–81.) Example:

> summarize.
> Let me ~~fill you in on the main points of the overall picture here.~~
> ^

1. At the present time, many different forms of hazing occur, such as various forms of physical abuse and also mental abuse.

2. Many people have a tendency toward the expansion of their sentences by the superfluous addition of extra words that are not really needed for the meaning of the sentences.

3. One of the major problems that is faced at this point in time is that there is world hunger.

4. After I stopped the practice of exercising regularly, I became ten pounds heavier in weight in a relatively short amount of time.

5. There are numerous theories that have been proposed by scientists as to why dinosaurs reached the point of becoming extinct.

6. At the present time, it is true and continues to remain the case that welfare reform is a really major, central, and important issue.

7. It is believed by many experts who have studied this problem that workers who labor on graveyard shifts exhibit a tendency to commit more errors than workers commit during the shift during the day.

8. Aaron requested of me and asked that in the event that he could not return to the campus by 9 A.M., at that point in time I ought to turn in his paper for him.

9. In the event that Britain had known of Hitler's plans at an earlier point in time, the war might have progressed in a different way.

10. The consensus of agreement that we have reached as a result of our discussions is that the paper originally scheduled on the calendar to be turned in on Monday will now be due on the following Friday thereafter.

14.2 Revising for conciseness

Revise the following paragraph so that each sentence is as concise as possible. Combine or divide sentences if necessary. (See *The Everyday Writer,* pp. 78–81.)

At the present time, one of the most serious problems that faces Americans in the area of public policy is the increasing rise in the cost of health care, which has occurred over an extended period of time. One major aspect of the severe crisis in health-care costs is that more and more expensive medical technology is being developed and marketed to doctors and hospitals. Even hospitals that are small in size want the latest kind of diagnostic device. The high cost of this expensive equipment is passed on to consumers, who are the patients. It is then passed on to insurance companies. Therefore, many employers are charging their employees more for health insurance because they themselves are having to pay higher and higher premiums. Others are reducing the employees' coverage to a significant extent. Meanwhile, almost forty million Americans suffer from the condition of a lack of any health insurance. In the event that they have an illness or an injury, they must go to a hospital emergency room. In large cities, emergency rooms are being overwhelmed by people seeking treatment for everything from life-threatening gunshot wounds to broken bones.

15.1   Varying sentence length

The following paragraph can be improved by varying sentence length. Read it aloud to get a sense of how it sounds. Then revise it, creating some short sentences and combining other sentences to create more effective long sentences. Add words or change punctuation as you need to. (See *The Everyday Writer,* pp. 81–83.)

Before beginning to play bridge, it is necessary to have the proper materials, the correct number of people, and a knowledge of the rank of suits and cards. The necessary materials include a full deck of playing cards (minus the jokers) and a score pad, along with a pen or pencil. Bridge is played by four people grouped into two partnerships, which are usually decided by drawing cards from a shuffled deck. The two players who draw the highest cards and the two who draw the lowest are partners, and the partners sit across from each other. The person who draws the highest card during partnership is the first dealer. Starting with the person on his or her left and going clockwise, the dealer deals each person one card at a time, face down. The deal continues until all four players have thirteen cards apiece. After the deal, the players sort their cards by suit, usually alternating black and red suits. The players then arrange the cards in ranking order from the highest, the ace, to the lowest, the deuce. The five highest cards, the ace, king, queen, jack, and ten, are referred to as honors. There is one suit that has great power and outranks every other one, the trump suit, which is designated at the start of the game.

Sentence Grammar

Identifying subjects and predicates

The following sentences are taken from "A Hanging" and "Shooting an Elephant," two essays by George Orwell. Identify the subject and the predicate in each sentence, underlining the subject once and the predicate twice. (See *The Everyday Writer*, pp. 96–100.) Example:

One <u>prisoner</u> <u>had been brought out of his cell.</u>

1. We set out for the gallows.

2. He was an army doctor, with a gray toothbrush moustache and a gruff voice.

3. The rest of us, magistrates and the like, followed behind.

4. The dog answered the sound with a whine.

5. The hangman, a gray-haired convict in the white uniform of the prison, was waiting beside his machine.

6. All this was perplexing and upsetting.

7. In a job like that, you see the dirty work of Empire at close quarters.

8. I had halted on the road.

9. It was an immense crowd, two thousand at the least and growing every minute.

10. His mouth slobbered.

16.2 Identifying verbs and verb phrases

Underline each verb or verb phrase in the following sentences. (See *The Everyday Writer,* pp. 98–101.) Example:

Terence <u>should sing</u> well in Sunday's performance.

1. My future does look bright.

2. The faucet had been leaking all day.

3. Within the next few weeks, we will receive the test results.

4. One person can collect sap, a second might run the evaporator, and a third should finish the syrup.

5. A job at an animal hospital would be great.

6. At a glittering ceremony, they announced the winner.

7. The gray whale has made a comeback and is beginning to flourish because of the intense efforts by preservationists.

8. The conference will include speakers from China, Brazil, and Japan.

9. We had been working ten-hour days.

10. Applicants must submit all required paperwork.

16.3 Identifying nouns and articles

Identify the nouns, including possessive forms, and the articles in each of the following sentences. Underline the nouns once and the articles twice. (See *The Everyday Writer,* pp. 89, 92.) Example:

<u><u>The</u> Puritans' hopes</u> were dashed when <u>Charles II</u> regained his

<u>father's throne.</u>

1. Nightlife begins in Georgetown even before the sun goes down.

2. Although plagiarism is dishonest and illegal, it does occur.

3. Thanksgiving is a grim season for turkeys.

4. Henderson's story is a tale of theft and violation.

5. In the front row sat two people, a man with slightly graying hair and a young woman in jeans.

6. The clock on the wall reads 2:15.

7. The cleaners finished your coat on Friday.

8. Alice, please tell me your secret.

9. I washed that mug already.

10. I chose broccoli over asparagus.

16.4 Identifying pronouns and antecedents

Identify the pronouns and any antecedents in each of the following sentences, underlining the pronouns once and any antecedents twice. (See *The Everyday Writer,* pp. 90–92.) Example:

As identical <u>twins</u>, <u>they</u> really do understand <u>each other</u>.

1. She thanked everyone for helping.

2. The crowd that greeted the pope was the largest one I have ever seen.

3. Who knows better than Mark himself what he should do?

4. They have only themselves to blame.

5. People who are extremely neat often annoy those who are not.

6. That cup, which you found on the coffee table, is mine.

7. Ron noticed his lawn was full of dandelions.

8. Everybody who is fascinated by cities should see New York.

9. The eagle that we sighted yesterday has its nest on Sauvie Island.

10. The senator likes herself too much for her own good.

16.5 Identifying adjectives and adverbs

Identify the adjectives and adverbs in each of the following sentences, underlining the adjectives once and the adverbs twice. Remember that articles and some pronouns can function as adjectives. (See *The Everyday Writer*, pp. 92–93.) Example:

Inadvertently, the two agents misquoted their major client.

1. Because time had grown perilously short, I quickly prepared the final draft.

2. Hilariously, the sly villain revealed himself at the end of the first act.

3. The somewhat shy author spoke reluctantly to six exuberant admirers.

4. I unhappily returned the sleek, new car to its owner.

5. The youngest dancer in the troupe performed a brilliant solo.

6. The most instructive of the books is, unfortunately, the longest.

7. Never before has one politician made a bigger mess in this amount of time.

8. Late in the day, the temperature dropped precipitously.

9. Imminent starvation threatens many populations constantly.

10. Politicians must seriously consider how well their lives will withstand intense public scrutiny.

16.6 Adding adjectives and adverbs

Expand each of the following sentences by adding appropriate adjectives and adverbs. Delete *the* if need be. (See *The Everyday Writer,* pp. 92–93.) Example:

> Then three   thoroughly   nervous
> ⌃The veterinarians examined the patient.
>   ⌃   ⌃   ⌃   ⌃

1. A corporation can fire workers.

2. The heroine marries the prince.

3. In the painting, a road curves between hills.

4. Candles gleamed on the tabletop.

5. Feminists have staged demonstrations against the movie.

6. Nobody saw the bear, but the ranger said it was dangerous.

7. Which way did you say the pair went?

8. Our assignment is due Wednesday.

9. Most of us enjoy movies.

10. Her superiors praised her work for the Environmental Protection Agency.

16.7 Identifying prepositions

Underline the prepositions in the following sentences. (See *The Everyday Writer,* pp. 93–94.) Example:

In the dim interior of the hut crouched an old man.

1. A gust of wind blew through the window, upsetting the vase on the table.

2. He ran swiftly around the brush, across the beach, and into the sea.

3. A few minutes past noon, the police arrived at the scene.

4. During our trip down the river, a rivalry developed between us.

5. The book, by Anne Morrow Lindbergh, describes the flight the Lindberghs made to the Orient by way of the Great Circle route.

6. According to your recent letter, the orders arrived on time.

7. Carry this painting down the hall, and leave it outside Gallery A.

8. For us, fifty dollars is a large sum of money.

9. Prepositions are combined with nouns to form prepositional phrases.

10. In each case, the preposition begins the phrase.

16.8 Identifying conjunctions

Underline the coordinating, correlative, and subordinating conjunctions as well as the conjunctive adverbs in each of the following sentences. Draw a connecting line to show both parts of any correlative conjunctions. (See *The Everyday Writer*, pp. 94–95.) Example:

We used sleeping bags <u>even though</u> the cabin had <u>both</u> sheets <u>and</u> blankets.

1. When we arrived at the pond, we saw many children playing there.

2. Pokey is an outside cat; nevertheless, she greets me at the front door each night as I arrive home.

3. The colt walked calmly, for he seemed to know he would win the race.

4. The shops along the waterfront were open, but business was slow.

5. The Environmental Protection Agency was once forced to buy an entire town because dioxins had rendered it uninhabitable.

6. The story was not only long but also dull.

7. I did not know whether to laugh or cry after I realized my mistake.

8. Exhausted men and women worked the pumps until their arms ached.

9. Although I live in a big city, my neighborhood has enough trees and raccoons to make me feel as though I live in the suburbs.

10. Neither Henry nor Rachel could understand the story; therefore, they did not recommend it.

16.9   Identifying conjunctions and interjections

Underline conjunctions once and interjections twice in each of the following sentences. Write COORD (for coordinating), CORREL (for correlative), or SUBORD (for subordinating) in parentheses after each sentence to indicate the types of conjunctions in use. (See *The Everyday Writer,* pp. 94–96.) Example:

> SUBORD
> <u>Hey</u>! <u>Unless</u> you turn the oven on, the cake won't bake!

1. Before you order dessert, make sure you have enough money to cover it.

2. After breakfast, either I'll rake the leaves, or I'll go for a walk.

3. Ouch! You pinched me, and I'm mad!

4. Jake and Sandy, Elly and Hank, and Sally Jo and Michael all plan to travel together and attend the conference.

5. Dee is arranging her schedule so that she can chair next week's meeting.

6. Our parts shipment did not arrive yesterday, so I cannot fill your order.

7. If you save money, you'll feel better both now and later.

8. Yeah. She said she likes you, but will she like your family?

9. You performed last night and still passed the test? Wow!

10. Until I saw that movie, I never thought about daily life at that time.

16.10 Identifying the parts of speech

For each underlined word in the following sentences, write its part of speech as it is used in the sentence. (See *The Everyday Writer,* pp. 89–96.) Example:

> ADJ N   PREP
> The <u>car</u> <u>door</u> slammed <u>into</u> the utility pole.

1. <u>Advertisements</u> clearly <u>and</u> directly reflect our sense of what we want.

2. One thing that Soloflex and NordicTrack and <u>Nike</u> agree on is that we <u>want</u> <u>fitness</u>.

3. And as the <u>frequency</u> of <u>movie</u> ads and music ads <u>suggests</u>, we <u>also</u> crave diversion: we want entertainment and relief <u>from</u> stress.

4. To get this <u>relief</u>, we <u>can</u> <u>purchase</u> a facsimile of <u>the</u> first edition of Ernest Hemingway's *For Whom the Bell Tolls.*

5. <u>Or</u> we can listen to the Beastie Boys' <u>popular</u> release *Ill Communication* from <u>Grand Royal</u> records.

6. <u>In</u> addition, advertisements suggest <u>that</u> we <u>consistently</u> worry about <u>our</u> health.

7. <u>So</u> we subscribe to newsletters describing the <u>latest</u> herbal extract or the latest all-natural vitamin <u>supplements</u>.

8. And, of course, we all <u>need</u> a new car, a "different kind of car," or a <u>truck</u> "<u>like</u> a rock."

9. Thinking <u>about</u> all these ads <u>makes</u> you wonder.

10. Maybe they <u>really</u> say more about the American economy than they do about the <u>actual</u> lives we <u>live</u>.

16.11 Identifying subjects

Identify the complete subject and the simple subject in each sentence. Underline the complete subject once and the simple subject twice. (See *The Everyday Writer*, p. 97.) Example:

The tall, powerful <u>woman</u> defiantly blocked the doorway.

1. The stories of Graham Greene probe the human psyche.

2. Has the new elevator been installed?

3. Here are some representative photographs.

4. The long, low, intricately carved table belonged to my aunt.

5. Some women worried about osteoporosis take calcium supplements.

6. Rap music has become both popular and controversial.

7. Bad spellers like my uncle are thankful for computer programs that can check spelling.

8. Television talk shows have become as popular as soap operas.

9. International travel, especially an extended stay in another country, almost always changes a person's view of home.

10. There's no time to study.

16.12 Identifying predicates

Underline the predicate in the following sentences. Then label each verb as linking, transitive, or intransitive. Finally, label all subject and object complements and all direct and indirect objects. (See *The Everyday Writer*, pp. 96–99.) Example:

TV   DO   OC
We <u>considered</u> <u>city life</u> <u>unbearable</u>.

1. Life is just a bowl of cherries.

2. The U.S. Constitution made us a nation.

3. A round of applause seemed appropriate.

4. Rock and roll will never die.

5. Advertisers promise consumers the world.

6. Jelly beans give Louise a toothache.

7. The candidate delivered an impassioned speech.

8. Candy tickled Lester under his arms.

9. The police officer tossed Ted his jacket.

10. Vincent's painting made everyone melancholy.

16.13 Identifying prepositional phrases

Following are some sentences written by the sports columnist Red Smith. Identify and underline all the prepositional phrases. Then choose two of the sentences, and for each, write a sentence that imitates its structure. (See *The Everyday Writer*, p. 100.) Example:

He glanced <u>about the room</u> <u>with a cocky, crooked grin</u>.

The cat stalked around the yard in her quiet, arrogant way.

1. In those days the Yankees always won the pennant.

2. Fear wasn't in his vocabulary and pain had no meaning.

3. Coaching in Columbus is not quite like coaching in New Haven.

4. He stepped out of the dugout and faced the multitude, two fists and one cap uplifted.

5. The old champ looked fit, square of shoulder and springy of tread, his skin clear, his eyes bright behind the glittering glasses.

16.14 Using prepositional phrases

Combine each of the following pairs of sentences into one sentence by making the second sentence into one or more prepositional phrases. (See *The Everyday Writer*, p. 100.) Example:

> over
> **The Greeks won a tremendous victory. ~~They were fighting~~ the**
>   ^
> **Persians.**

1. Socrates was condemned. His fellow citizens made up the jury that condemned him.

2. Socrates faced death. He had no fear.

3. The playwright Aristophanes wrote a comedy. Its subject was Socrates.

4. Everyone thought Socrates was crazy. Only a few followers disagreed.

5. Today Socrates is honored. He founded Western philosophy.

6. The treatment Socrates received appalled some contemporaries. It appalled Plato.

7. When Plato was a boy, he knew the older Socrates. Athens was Plato's boyhood home.

8. Socrates was Plato's teacher. He taught Plato philosophy.

9. Later Plato opened the Academy. It was his own school.

10. Plato wrote the *Republic*. The *Republic* is a dialogue.

16.15 Identifying verbal phrases

Identify each participial phrase, gerund phrase, and infinitive phrase. Identify any sentence in which the verbal phrase acts as the subject of the sentence. (See *The Everyday Writer*, p. 101.) Example:

┌────── PARTICIPIAL ──────┐
Pacing the hall with impatience, I wished my friends would

arrive.

1. Buying his first Corvette was the happiest moment in Brendan's life.

2. After four years of careful saving, he got his car.

3. Our plan was to renovate the house and then to sell it.

4. Raised in Idaho, I spent plenty of time exploring nature.

5. Sitting by the window and listening to the wind blowing through the trees, I feel happy and lucky to be alive.

6. Feeling ill, Rob called to cancel his date with Monica.

7. Named by the railroad, Havre, Malta, and Glasgow can all be found in Montana.

8. Swimming every other morning keeps Toni fit.

9. A chef specializing in American cooking is taking over the food service.

10. With ears ringing loudly and feet aching mightily, I left the concert and headed for my car.

16.16 Identifying prepositional, verbal, absolute, and appositive phrases

Read the following sentences, and identify and label all the prepositional, verbal, absolute, and appositive phrases. Notice that one kind of phrase may appear within another kind. (See *The Everyday Writer,* pp. 100–102.) Example:

```
        ┌──────── ABSOLUTE ────────┐              ┌── PREP ──┐
        His voice breaking with emotion, Ed thanked us for the award.
                    └── PREP ──┘
        └ VERBAL ──────────────┘
```

1. Approaching the rope, I suddenly fell into the icy pond.

2. To listen to Patsy Cline is sheer delight.

3. The figure outlined against the sky seemed unable to move.

4. Floating on my back, I ignored my practice requirements.

5. Jane stood still, her fingers clutching the fence.

6. Bobby, a sensitive child, was filled with a mixture of awe and excitement.

7. Shocked into silence, they kept their gaze fixed on the odd creature.

8. Basking in the sunlight, I was lost in reminiscence of birch trees.

9. Anna, the leader of the group, was reluctant to relinquish any authority.

10. His favorite form of recreation was taking a nap.

16.17 Adding prepositional, verbal, absolute, and appositive phrases

Use prepositional, participial, infinitive, gerund, absolute, or appositive phrases to expand each of the following sentences. (See *The Everyday Writer,* pp. 100–102.) Example:

In response to a vigorous shake,
The apples dropped from the limb.

1. Nancy jogged down Willow Street.

2. She looked healthy when he saw her the second time.

3. Tomás had lost almost all his hair.

4. The Sunday afternoon dragged.

5. Teresa looked at her mother.

6. The candidates shook hands with the voters.

7. We were uncertain what to do.

8. Ben often thought regretfully about the past.

9. The letter lay on the desk.

10. They lived in a trailer.

16.18 Using verbal, absolute, and appositive phrases to combine sentences

Use a participial, infinitive, gerund, absolute, or appositive phrase to combine each of the following pairs of sentences into one sentence. (See *The Everyday Writer*, pp. 101–102.) Example:

His constant complaining
He complained constantly. This habit irritated his coworkers.
^

1. David Klein performed a monologue. He is an actor and comedian.

2. We waited to go through customs. Our passports were in our hands.

3. She bought a new camera. This purchase lifted her spirits.

4. He relied too much on his computer. That dependence was his downfall.

5. The protesters were carrying their banners. They headed down the street.

6. The large American cockroach's other names are Palmetto bug and water bug. It likes moist environments.

7. Have you heard about poisonous cone snails? They live in the Philippines.

8. His concentration on his experiments is intense. He blocks out the rest of the world.

9. City-dwellers sunbathe on apartment-building roofs. The roofs are known as "tar beach."

10. They both need to use the computer. It is a laptop.

16.19 Identifying dependent clauses

Underline dependent clauses, and label any subordinating conjunctions and relative pronouns in each of the following sentences. (See *The Everyday Writer*, pp. 102–103.) Example:

SUB CONJ
If I were going on an overnight hike, I would carry a lightweight stove.

1. The driver who won the race was driving a tan Pontiac.

2. As a potential customer entered the store, Tony nervously attempted to retreat to the safety of the back room.

3. The names they called my grandmother still haunt me.

4. When she was deemed old enough to understand, she was told the truth, and she finally learned that her father had left home, not died.

5. Though most of my grandfather's farm was wooded, there were also great expanses of green lawns with quiet, trickling streams.

6. I decided to bake a chocolate-cream pie, which was Lynn's favorite.

7. If Keats had lived longer, he might have written even greater poems, but his early death is perhaps part of his appeal.

8. The trip was longer than I had remembered.

9. After she finished the painting, Linda cleaned the brushes.

10. I could see that he was extremely tired, but I had to ask him a few questions.

16.20 Adding dependent clauses

Expand each of the following sentences by adding at least one dependent clause to it. Be prepared to explain how your addition improves the sentence. (See *The Everyday Writer*, pp. 102–103.) Example:

> As the earth continued to shake,
> **The books tumbled from the shelves.**

1. The last guests left.

2. The German government dismantled the Berlin Wall.

3. The new computer made a strange noise.

4. Rob always borrowed money from friends.

5. The streets were ringing with loud music.

6. We stood outside for an hour.

7. The history seminar begins tomorrow.

8. Erin won the translation contest.

9. A river had flowed through the forest.

10. A man was killed in that mill in 1867.

16.21   Distinguishing between phrases and clauses

The following are some sentences from the letters of E. B. White. Read each one carefully, focusing on the phrases and clauses. Underline any dependent clauses once and any phrases twice. Identify each phrase as a prepositional phrase or a verbal phrase. Finally, choose two sentences, and use them as a model for sentences of your own, imitating White's structure phrase for phrase and clause for clause. (See *The Everyday Writer,* pp. 100–104.) Example:

> I was born **in 1899** and expect **to live forever, searching for beauty** and **raising hell in general**.
>
> PREPOSITIONAL PHRASES: in 1899, for beauty, in general
> VERBAL PHRASES: to live forever, searching for beauty, raising hell
> IMITATION SENTENCE: Sarah was hired in May and plans to work all summer, living at home and saving money for law school.

1. You can see at a glance that Professor Strunk omitted needless words.

2. Either Macmillan takes Strunk and me in our bare skins, or I want out.

3. I regard the word *hopefully* as beyond recall.

4. Life in a zoo is just the ticket for some animals and birds.

5. I recall the pleasures and satisfactions of encountering a Perelman piece in a magazine.

6. The way to read Thoreau is to enjoy him—his enthusiasms, his acute perception.

7. When I start a book, I never know what my characters are going to do, and I accept no responsibility for their eccentric behavior.

8. No sensible writer sets out deliberately to develop a style, but all writers do have distinguishing qualities, and they become very evident when you read the words.

9. When I wrote "Death of a Pig," I was simply rendering an account of what actually happened on my place—to my pig, who died, and to me, who tended him in his last hours.

10. A good many of Charlotte's descendants still live in the barn, and when the warm days of spring arrive there will be lots of tiny spiders emerging into the world.

16.22 Classifying sentences grammatically and functionally

Classify each of the following sentences as simple, compound, complex, or compound-complex. In addition, note any sentences that could be classified as declarative, imperative, interrogative, or exclamatory. (See *The Everyday Writer*, pp. 104–105.) Example:

Stop the thief! simple, imperative

1. Solve your problems yourself.

2. The screen door creaked and banged when she ran into the house.

3. Should he admit his mistake, or should he keep quiet and hope to avoid discovery?

4. People go on safari to watch wild animals in their natural habitat.

5. When I first arrived at college, I became confused about where I fit in and who my role models should be.

6. Keeping in mind the terrain, the weather, and the length of the hike, decide what you need to take.

7. Dreams are necessary, but they can be frustrating unless you have the means to attain them.

8. Retail sales declined as consumers cut back on discretionary spending, and many small businesses failed.

9. Oh, I detest jokes at other people's expense!

10. Or is telling such jokes a human trait that we can't eliminate?

17.1   Using irregular verb forms

Complete each of the following sentences by filling in each blank with the past tense or past participle of the verb listed in parentheses. (See *The Everyday Writer*, pp. 108–112. Example:

They had already _____ *eaten* _____ (eat) the beef; later they

_____ *ate* _____ (eat) the ham.

1. Clearly this short story would not have _____ (be) so effective if it had been _____ (write) in the third person.

2. After she had _____ (make) her decision, she _____ (find) that the constant anxiety was no longer a factor in her daily life.

3. The process of hazing _____ (begin) soon after fraternities were formed.

4. Hearns _____ (lose) control of the fight, and Nolan _____ (take) advantage of this loss.

5. When Maria Callas _____ (make) her debut at the Metropolitan Opera, some people _____ (know) that music history was being made.

6. Katherine Dunn, an unorthodox novelist who _____
   (choose) thorny subjects, has now _____ (become) a cause
   for some dedicated readers.

7. Reluctantly, Marisol _____ (shake) her head in disagree-
   ment; she had _____ (bring) with her the necessary evi-
   dence to disprove John's claim.

8. Roberto had _____ (throw) his hat into the ring and had
   assembled the best advisors he had _____ (be) able to find.

9. When Charles admitted that he had _____ (break) into the
   apartment, he said that he had _____ (lose) his keys.

10. I discovered that I had _____ (fall) into a rut; for several
    months I had neither _____ (break) my routines nor
    _____ (do) anything new.

17.2 Editing verb forms

Where necessary, edit the following sentences to eliminate any inappropriate verb forms. If the verb forms in a sentence are appropriate
as printed, write C. (See *The Everyday Writer*, pp. 108–112.) Example:

> began
> She ~~begin~~ the examination on time.
>   ^

1. Socrates drank the hemlock calmly and died a few hours later.

2. The band had sang its last song before the fight begun.

3. When the battle was over, the rebels had been beat badly.

4. By the mid-1970s, New York had almost went bankrupt.

5. The lake froze early this year.

6. We brung baked beans to the potluck dinner.

7. Over the years, Martin has become a close friend.

8. They had rode sidesaddle before.

9. They had felt that tired only once before.

10. They had drank too much before I even arrived.

17.3 Distinguishing between *lie* and *lay, sit* and *set, rise* and *raise*

Choose the appropriate verb form in each of the following sentences. (See *The Everyday Writer*, p. 112.) Example:

She <u>sat</u>/set in the rocking chair, daydreaming.

1. Sometimes she just lies/lays and stares at the ceiling.

2. I lay/laid my books down just as the telephone rang.

3. As the flag rose/raised, a trumpeter played "Taps."

4. He used whatever was lying/laying around the house.

5. Doctors urge us to sit/set aside fad diets once and for all.

6. I sat/set back, closed my eyes, and began to meditate.

7. Sitting/Setting in the sun too long can lead to skin cancer.

8. The Federal Reserve Bank is planning to rise/raise interest rates.

9. In this area, when the temperature rises/raises, the humidity usually declines.

10. We rose/raised every morning at six and went jogging.

17.4 Deciding on verb tenses

Complete each of the following sentences by filling in the blank with an appropriate form of the verb given in parentheses. Since more than one form will sometimes be possible, be prepared to explain the reasons for your choices. (See *The Everyday Writer*, pp. 112–116.) Example:

In the 1980s, many of the baby boomers _____*became*_____ **(become)**

parents.

1. In spite of the poor turnout for today's referendum, local officials

   _____ (expect) the bond issue to pass.

2. Ever since the first nuclear power plants were built, opponents

   _____ (predict) disaster.

3. Thousands of Irish peasants _____ (emigrate) to America

   after the potato famine of the 1840s.

4. The newspaper _____ (arrive) by the time I awake.

5. The committee _____ (meet) again next week.

6. President Kennedy was shot while he _____ (ride) in a

   limousine.

7. Antiabortion activists _____ (try) to reverse the decision.

8. By the time a child born today enters first grade, he or she

   _____ (watch) thousands of television commercials.

9. In "The Road Not Taken," the speaker _____ (come) to a

   fork in the road.

10. The supply of a product _____ (rise) when the demand is

    great.

17.5 Sequencing tenses

Change the italicized word or phrase in each of the following sentences to create the appropriate sequence of tenses. If a sentence reads acceptably, write *A*. (See *The Everyday Writer,* p. 116.) Example:

> He needs *to* s̶e̶n̶d̶ in his application before today.
>
> (have sent)

1. When he was twenty-one, he *wanted to have become* a millionaire by the age of thirty.

2. *Leaving* England in December, the settlers arrived in Virginia in May.

3. They *hoped* to plant their garden by now.

4. *Cutting off* all contact with family, he did not know whom to ask for help.

5. *Having sung* in the shower, he did not hear the doorbell.

6. Mitch Williams threw a curve even though the catcher *will signal* a fast ball.

7. The crew *had dug* the trench before they installed the cable.

8. The news had just begun when our power *goes* out.

9. Ulla *will have returned* to Denmark by the time you arrive home.

10. Will you tell Grandpa about your wedding plans when he *has visited* us in the summer?

17.6 Converting the voice of a sentence

Convert each sentence from active to passive voice or from passive to active, and note the differences in emphasis these changes make. (See *The Everyday Writer,* pp. 116–117.) Example:

> **Machiavelli advises the prince to gain the friendship of the people.**
>
> The prince is advised by Machiavelli to gain the friendship of the people.

1. Huge pine trees were uprooted by the storm.

2. Marianne avoided such things as elevators, subways, and closets.

3. For months, the baby kangaroo is protected, fed, and taught how to survive by its mother.

4. The lawns and rooftops were covered with the first snow of winter.

5. Flannery O'Connor employs the images of both a boxcar and a swinging bridge to show the inconsistencies between Mrs. Turpin's classification of people and God's classification of people.

6. The experimental data are analyzed in the next section of this report.

7. Suddenly, rainfall pounded on the roof over our heads.

8. The last doughnut in the box was eaten by Jerry just a few minutes ago.

9. The play was directed wonderfully by Mr. Wallcrown.

10. Has Moira told you about our house rules?

17.7 Using subjunctive mood

Revise any of the following sentences that do not use the appropriate subjunctive verb forms required in formal or academic writing. (See *The Everyday Writer,* pp. 117–119.) Example:

were
I saw how carefully he moved, as if he ~~was~~ caring for an infant.
                                                    ^

1. Her stepsisters treated Cinderella as though she was a servant.

2. Hamlet wishes he was not responsible for avenging his murdered father.

3. Freud recommended that an analyst use dreams as a means of studying the human personality.

4. If more money was available, we would be able to offer more student scholarships.

5. It is necessary that the manager knows how to do any job in the store.

6. If Lamont were here, he would know what to do.

7. The lawyer made it seem as if I was a threat to society.

8. The only requirement is that the tense of both clauses makes sense.

9. I wish I was with you right now.

10. It is requested that each member contributes ten dollars.

18.1　Selecting verbs that agree with their subjects

Underline the appropriate verb form in each of the following sentences. (See *The Everyday Writer,* pp. 119–125.) Example:

The benefits of family planning is/<u>are</u> not apparent to many people.

1. Starving children and world peace is/are two of my concerns.

2. Dershowitz, together with his aide, presents/present a cogent argument.

3. Walls of glass characterizes/characterize much modern architecture.

4. The system of sororities and fraternities supplies/supply much of the social life on some college campuses.

5. The buck stops/stop here.

6. The first baseman, along with the shortstop, is/are being traded to San Diego.

7. In many species, the male, as well as the female, cares/care for the offspring.

8. He holds/hold a controlling interest in the company.

9. The author of those stories writes/write beautifully.

10. Current research on that disease, in spite of the best efforts of hundreds of scientists, leaves/leave serious questions unanswered.

18.2 Making subjects and verbs agree

Revise any of the following sentences as necessary to establish subject-verb agreement. Some sentences do not require any change. (See *The Everyday Writer*, pp. 119–125.) Example:

Into the shadows dart̂ the frightened raccoon.

1. Every check and money order cost fifty cents.

2. Talking and getting up from my seat was my crime.

3. If rhythm and blues is your kind of music, try Mary Lou's.

4. His merry disposition and his recognized success in business make him popular in the community.

5. *The vapors* were a Victorian term for hypochondria.

6. Neither the lighting nor the frame display the painting well.

7. In the foreground is two women playing musical instruments.

8. Most of the voters support a reduction in nuclear weapons.

9. Each of the entrants rehearse for a minimum of three hours daily.

10. Neither her manner nor her tantrums intimidates the staff.

11. The audience as a whole always respond to Pavarotti.

12. My grandmother is the only one of my relatives who still goes to church.

13. *Our Tapes* were one of Fitzgerald's earlier titles for *Tender Is the Night.*

14. Sweden was one of the few European countries that was neutral in 1943.

15. Politics have been defined as the art of the possible.

19.1　Using adjectives and adverbs appropriately

Revise each of the following sentences to maintain correct adverb and adjective use. Then, for each adjective and adverb you've revised, point out the word that it modifies. (See *The Everyday Writer,* pp. 125–130.) Example:

The attorney delivered a ~~superb~~ conceived summation. *superbly*

1. Honest lawyers are not complete obsessed with status or money.

2. First he acts negative toward her, and then, in the next episode, he proposes marriage!

3. Hypochondriacs call a doctor whenever they feel badly.

4. Christmas Day was real cold, and it was raining heavy.

5. The executive spoke forceful about the new union regulations.

6. Regrettably, the youngster was hurt bad in the accident.

7. The skater performed good despite the intense competition.

8. The instructor felt well about her presentation.

9. On the new stereo, many of the CDs, records, and tapes sounded differently.

10. They brought up their children very strict.

19.2 Using comparative and superlative modifiers appropriately

Revise each of the following sentences to use modifiers correctly, clearly, and effectively. A variety of acceptable answers is possible for each sentence. (See *The Everyday Writer*, pp. 128–130.) Example:

> **In the Macbeths' marriage, Lady Macbeth is presented as the ~~most~~ ambitious of the two.**

1. She has the most unique laugh.

2. The trainer is more gentler with first-time exercisers.

3. St. Francis made Assisi one of the famousest towns in Italy.

4. Most of the elderly are women because women tend to live longer.

5. Minneapolis is the largest of the Twin Cities.

6. The Van Gogh painting was the most priceless.

7. My graduation day will be the most happiest day of my life.

8. Although the prices were close at all three pizzerias, Pizza Gallery's were lower.

9. Japanese cars captured much of the American market because American consumers found they were more reliable.

10. I think *Oedipus Rex* is a successfuler play than *The Sandbox*.

20.1 Revising sentences with misplaced modifiers

Revise each of the following sentences by moving any misplaced modifiers so that they clearly modify the words they are intended to. You may have to change grammatical structures for some sentences. (See *The Everyday Writer,* pp. 130–133.) Example:

> **Elderly people and students live in the neighborhood**
> full of identical tract houses
> **surrounding the university/.which is full of identical tract houses.**
> ^   ^

1. The tenor captivated the entire audience singing with verve.

2. The city almost spent two million dollars on the new stadium.

3. On the day in question, the patient was not normally able to breathe.

4. The clothes were full of holes that I was giving away.

5. Politicians are supported by the people when they propose sensible plans.

6. Doctors recommend a new test for cancer, which is painless.

7. I went through the process of taxiing and taking off in my mind.

8. I knew that the investment would pay off in a dramatic way before I decided to buy the stock.

9. The bank offered flood insurance to the homeowners underwritten by the federal government.

10. Revolving out of control, the maintenance worker shut down the turbine.

20.2 Revising squinting modifiers, disruptive modifiers, and split infinitives

Revise each of the following sentences by moving disruptive modifiers and split infinitives as well as by repositioning any squinting modifier so that it unambiguously modifies either the word(s) before it or the word(s) after it. You may have to add words to a sentence to revise it adequately. (See *The Everyday Writer*, p. 132.) Example:

The course we hoped would engross us completely bored us.

The course we hoped would completely engross us bored us.
OR
The course we hoped would engross us bored us completely.

1. He remembered vividly enjoying the sound of Mrs. McIntosh's singing.

2. The mayor promised after her reelection she would not raise taxes.

3. The collector who owned the painting originally planned to leave it to a museum.

4. Doctors can now restore limbs that have been severed partially to a functioning condition.

5. The speaker said when he finished he would answer questions.

6. Eastern North America was, when Europeans arrived, covered in forest.

7. The exhibit, because of extensive publicity, attracted large audiences.

8. The architect wanted to eventually responsibly design public buildings.

9. Bookstores sold, in the first week after publication, fifty thousand copies.

10. The stock exchange became, because of the sudden trading, a chaotic circus.

11. The state commission promised at its final meeting to make its recommendations public.

12. Rico felt after eating two chicken breasts, a baked potato, a tossed salad, and strawberry shortcake full.

13. In the next several months, Lynn hopes to despite her busy schedule of entertaining maintain her diet and actually lose weight.

14. She sang in her first public concert a selection of traditional folk songs and ballads.

15. People who swim frequently will improve their physical condition.

20.3 Revising dangling modifiers

Revise each of the following sentences to correct the dangling modifiers. (See *The Everyday Writer,* p. 133.) Example:

a viewer gets
Watching television news, an impression is given of constant disaster.

1. High ratings are pursued by emphasizing fires and murders.

2. Interviewing grieving relatives, no consideration is shown for their privacy.

3. To provide comic relief, heat waves and blizzards are attributed to the weather forecaster.

4. Chosen for their looks, the newscasters' journalistic credentials are often weak.

5. As a visual medium, complex issues are hard to present in a televised format.

6. However unhappy, my part-time job is something I have to put up with.

7. While attending a performance at Ford's Theater, Booth shot Lincoln.

8. A waiter's job can become very stressful when faced with a busy restaurant full of hungry people.

9. Dreams are somewhat like a jigsaw puzzle; if put together in the correct order, organization and coherence become obvious.

10. No matter how costly, my family insists on a college education.

11. Singing in the shower, the water suddenly turned cold.

12. Dressed and ready for the dance, her car would not start.

13. Whenever driving, your seat belt should be fastened.

14. While cycling through southern France, the Roman ruins impressed me.

15. After swimming for an hour, lunch was delayed.

21.1 Using subjective case pronouns

Replace the underlined noun or nouns in each of the following sentences with the appropriate subjective case pronoun. (See *The Everyday Writer,* p. 135.) Example:

> he
> Jack and ~~George~~ visited the new science library.
> ^

1. Whenever <u>Jerry, David, and Sean</u> went to the beach, the weather was bad.

2. As the cattle crossed the road, <u>the cattle</u> stopped all traffic.

3. The rhododendrons are most beautiful in May when <u>the rhododendrons</u> bloom.

4. <u>Jody, Susan, Scott, and I</u> were the only people still in the building.

5. Maya wondered if <u>Maya</u> were smarter than James.

6. The person who got the highest mark on the test was <u>Susan</u>.

7. Joel was curious to see whether or not <u>Joel</u> would be asked to work late.

8. Justin, Paolo, and I have a great time whenever <u>Justin, Paolo, and I</u> get together.

9. The cars slowed to a stop whenever <u>the cars</u> approached an on-ramp.

10. John said that the largest contributors were <u>John</u> and I.

21.2 Using objective case pronouns

Most of the following sentences use pronouns incorrectly. Revise the incorrect sentences so that they contain correct objective case pronouns. (See *The Everyday Writer,* p. 136.) Example:

                                       me

Eventually, the headwaiter told Kim, Stanley, and ̶I̶ that we could be seated.

1. Between you and I, that essay doesn't deserve a high grade.

2. Cycling thirty miles a day was triathlon training for Bill, Ubijo, and I.

3. Though even the idea of hang gliding made herself nervous, she gave it a try.

4. Which of those books is for myself?

5. Which of the twins are you waiting for—Mary or he?

6. We need two volunteers: yourself and Tom.

7. The supervisor persuaded me and they to work late.

8. Remembering him fondly, I cried throughout the funeral.

9. Give he what he deserves.

10. The president gave her the highest praise.

21.3 Using possessive case pronouns

Insert a possessive pronoun in the blank in each sentence. (See *The Everyday Writer*, p. 136.) Example:

_____My_____ **eyes ached after studying for ten hours.**

1. Your parents must be pleased about _____ going back to college.

2. Ken's dinner arrived quickly, but Rose waited an hour for

   _____ .

3. We agreed to pool _____ knowledge.

4. Even many supporters of Lincoln opposed _____ freeing the slaves.

5. _____ responsibility should it be to teach moral values?

6. The green marker is yours; the red one is _____ .

7. You may not use my computer. I repeat: it's _____ .

8. Jean basted the turkey so that _____ skin would not dry out.

9. Many fans of Tom Hanks's recall _____ acting in *Big*.

10. After slipping on marbles, the mother gathered them and asked her twin sons, " _____ are these?"

21.4 Using *who, whoever, whom,* or *whomever*

Insert *who, whoever, whom,* or *whomever* appropriately in the blank in each of the following sentences. (See *The Everyday Writer,* pp. 136–138.) Example:

She is someone _____ who _____ will go far.

1. _____ shall I say is calling?

2. _____ the voters choose faces an almost impossible challenge.

3. The manager promised to reward _____ sold the most cars.

4. Professor Quinones asked _____ we wanted to collaborate with.

5. _____ will the new tax law benefit most?

6. Soap operas appeal to _____ is interested in intrigue, suspense, joy, pain, grief, romance, fidelity, sex, and violence.

7. The only experts _____ they can recommend are the two magicians who trained them.

8. Richard said he'd be glad to speak to _____ showed up to listen.

9. She shared the secret with those _____ she trusted.

10. _____ he instructed to write this report certainly did not do a thorough job.

21.5 Using pronouns in compound structures, appositives, elliptical clauses; choosing between *we* and *us* before a noun

Choose the appropriate pronoun from the pair in parentheses in each of the following sentences. (See *The Everyday Writer*, pp. 138–140.) Example:

Of the group, only (<u>she</u>/her) and I finished the race.

1. The relationship between (they/them) and their brother was often strained.

2. Only (he/him), a few cabinet members, and several military leaders were aware of the steady advance the enemy was making.

3. At the time, I had three friends who were indeed stronger, better looking, and more popular than (I/me).

4. The only candidates left in the race were (he/him) and Clinton.

5. All the other job applicants were far more experienced than (I/me).

6. When Jessica and (she/her) first met, they despised each other.

7. The two violinists, Sergei and (he/him), played as though they had a single musical mind.

8. To (we/us) New Englanders, hurricanes are a bigger worry than tornadoes.

9. Tomorrow (we/us) raw recruits will have our first on-the-job test.

10. Talking first of the deep trust he felt for his own father and then trying to compliment me, Ken went on to say, "I trust you as much as (he/him)."

11. The readers (she and I/her and me), agreed that the story was very suspenseful.

12. Just between you and (I/me), this seminar is a disaster!

13. Staying a week in a lakeside cabin gave (we/us) New Yorkers a much-needed vacation.

14. Lute Johannson always claimed he was the best of (we/us) chili cookers.

15. Jason is younger than (I/me).

21.6 Maintaining pronoun-antecedent agreement

Revise the following sentences as needed to create pronoun-antecedent agreement and to eliminate the generic *he* and any awkward pronoun references. Some sentences can be revised in more than one way, and one sentence does not require any change. (See *The Everyday Writer*, pp. 141–143.) Example:

Every graduate submitted his diploma card.

Every graduate submitted his or her diploma card.

All graduates submitted their diploma cards.

1. With tuition on the rise, a student has to save money wherever they can.

2. Not everyone gets along with his roommate, but the two can usually manage to tolerate each other temporarily.

3. Congress usually resists presidential attempts to encroach on what they consider their authority.

4. Either Jack or Jill are always falling down hills.

5. If his own knowledge is all the reader has to go by, how can he identify one source as more reliable than another?

6. Every house and apartment has their advantages and their drawbacks.

7. Neither the scouts nor their leader knew their way out of the forest.

8. Our team no longer wears its red uniforms.

9. To create a positive impression, a candidate attempts to flood the media with favorable publicity about themselves.

10. I often turn on the fan and the light and neglect to turn it off.

21.7 Clarifying pronoun reference

Revise each of the following sentences to clarify pronoun reference. All the items can be revised in more than one way. If a pronoun refers ambiguously to more than one possible antecedent, revise the sentence in at least two different ways, reflecting each possible meaning. (See *The Everyday Writer*, pp. 141–143.) Example:

After Jane left, Miranda found her keys.

Miranda found Jane's keys after Jane left.

Miranda found her own keys after Jane left.

1. Anna smiled at her mother as she opened the birthday package.

2. Lear divides his kingdom between the two older daughters, Goneril and Regan, whose extravagant professions of love are more flattering than the simple affection of the youngest daughter, Cordelia. The consequences of this error in judgment soon become apparent, as they prove neither grateful nor kind to him.

3. The tragedy of child abuse is that even after the children of abusive parents grow up, they often continue the sad tradition of cruelty.

4. New England helped shape many aspects of American culture, including education, religion, and government. As New Englanders moved west, they carried its institutions with them.

5. Ira told Ed he needed a vacation.

6. Bill smilingly announced his promotion to Ed.

7. After Ed hired Paul, he felt relieved.

8. When drug therapy is combined with psychotherapy, the patients relate better to their therapists, are less vulnerable to what disturbs them, and are more responsive to them.

9. Not long after the company set up the subsidiary, it went bankrupt.

10. Quint trusted Smith because she had worked for her before.

21.8   Revising to clarify pronoun reference

Revise the following paragraph to establish a clear antecedent for every pronoun that needs one. (See *The Everyday Writer,* pp. 141–143.)

In Paul Fussell's essay "My War," he writes about his experience in combat during World War II, which he says still haunts his life. Fussell confesses that he joined the infantry ROTC in 1939 as a way of getting out of gym class, where he would have been forced to expose his "fat and flabby" body to the ridicule of his classmates. However, it proved to be a serious miscalculation. After the United States entered the war in 1941, other male college students were able to join officer training programs in specialized fields that kept them out of combat. If you were already in an ROTC unit associated with the infantry, though, you were trapped in it. That was how

Fussell came to be shipped to France as a rifle-platoon leader in 1944. Almost immediately they sent him to the front, where he soon developed pneumonia because of insufficient winter clothing. He spent a month in hospitals; because he did not want to worry his parents, however, he told them it was just the flu. When he returned to the front, he was wounded by a shell that killed his sergeant.

22.1   Revising comma splices and fused sentences

Revise each of the following comma splices or fused sentences using any two of these five methods:

Separate the clauses into two sentences.

Link clauses with a comma and a coordinating conjunction.

Link clauses with a semicolon and, perhaps, a conjunctive adverb or a transitional phrase.

Recast the two clauses as one independent clause.

Recast one independent clause as a dependent clause.

Use each of the methods at least once. (See *The Everyday Writer*, pp. 143–148.) Example:

> **I had misgivings about the marriage, I did not attend the ceremony.**
>
> I had misgivings about the marriage, so I did not attend the ceremony.
>
> Because I had misgivings about the marriage, I did not attend the ceremony.

1. I was sitting on a log bridge, the sun sank low in the sky.

2. Reporters today have no choice they must use computers.

3. I completed the test, I was uncertain about the last essay question.

4. My mother taught me to read my grandmother taught me to *love* to read.

5. *David Copperfield* was written as a serial it is ideal for television.

6. Lincoln called for troops to fight the Confederacy, four more southern states seceded as a result.

7. The California condor is almost extinct scientists are trying to save it.

8. E. B. White died in 1985 his work continues to inspire readers.

9. Václav Havel was once imprisoned as a dissident, still, he eventually became president of Czechoslovakia.

10. The music lifted her spirits she stopped sighing and began to sing.

11. Fashion designing demands a rigorous knowledge of fabric, of the human form, and of changing taste, it also demands daring, intuition, and an eagerness to set fashion rather than follow it.

12. One month she can't talk or even sit up by herself, she's standing wobbly-legged against the furniture and calling, "Ma, Ma."

13. She awoke feeling unusually optimistic she felt as though she might sing out loud.

14. The college of education receives applications from more individuals than it can admit the college carefully screens all applications.

15. No rain fell in Iowa for more than six weeks, grain and corn farmers suffered significant losses.

16. Perhaps this whole thing is a joke then, again, maybe it isn't.

17. Gumbo is well worth all the trouble, it takes a long time to prepare.

18. The concert was sold out the promoters added another show.

19. Computer technology changes rapidly, however few businesses can afford to take advantage of every new advance.

20. Our diplomatic efforts failed, then we prepared for war.

22.2   Revising comma splices

Revise the following paragraph, eliminating all comma splices by using a period or a semicolon. Then revise the paragraph again, this time using any of these three methods:

Separate independent clauses into sentences of their own.

Recast two or more clauses as one independent clause.

Recast one independent clause as a dependent clause.

Comment on the two revisions. What differences in rhythm do you detect? Which version do you prefer, and why? (See *The Everyday Writer*, pp. 143–148.)

My sister Mary decided to paint her house last summer, thus, she had to buy some paint. She wanted inexpensive paint, at the same time, it had to go on easily and cover well, that combination was unrealistic to start with. She had never done exterior painting before, in fact, she did not even own a ladder. She was a complete beginner, on the other hand, she was a hard worker and was willing to learn. She got her husband, Dan, to take a week off from work, likewise she let her two teen-age sons take three days off from school to help. Mary went out and bought the "dark green" paint for $6.99 a gallon, it must have been mostly water, in fact, you could almost see through it. Mary and Dan and the boys put one coat of this paint on the house, as a result, their white house turned a streaky light green. Dan and the boys rebelled, declaring they would not work anymore with such cheap paint. Mary was forced to buy all new paint, even so, the house did not really get painted until September.

22.3 Revising comma splices and fused sentences

Revise the following paragraph, eliminating the comma splices and fused sentences using any of these methods:

Separate independent clauses into sentences of their own.

Link clauses with a comma and a coordinating conjunction.

Link clauses with a semicolon and, perhaps, a conjunctive adverb or a transitional phrase.

Recast two or more clauses as one independent clause.

Recast one independent clause as a dependent clause.

Then revise the paragraph again, this time eliminating each comma splice and fused sentence by a different method. Decide which paragraph is more effective, and why. Finally, compare the revision you prefer with the revisions of several other students, and discuss the ways in which the versions differ in meaning. (See *The Everyday Writer,* pp. 143–148.)

Gardening can be very satisfying, it is also hard work people who just see the pretty flowers may not realize this. The whole garden area has to be rototilled every year, this process is not much like the ad showing people walking quietly behind the rototiller, on the contrary, my father has to fight that machine every inch of the way, sweating so much he looks like Hulk Hogan after a hard bout, then the planting all must be done by hand, my back aches, my hands get raw, my skin gets sunburned. I get filthy whenever I go near that garden my mother always asks me to help, though. When harvest time comes, the effort is *almost* worth it, however, there are always extra zucchinis I give away at school or the office everybody else is trying to give away zucchinis, too. We also have tomatoes, lettuce, there is always more than we need and we feel bad wasting it wouldn't you like this nice bag of cucumbers?

23.1 Eliminating sentence fragments

Revise each of the following fragments, either by combining fragments with independent clauses or by rewriting them as separate sentences. (See *The Everyday Writer,* pp. 148–152.) Example:

Zoe looked close to tears. Standing with her head bowed.

Standing with her head bowed, Zoe looked close to tears.

Zoe looked close to tears. She was standing with her head bowed.

1. Small, long-veined, fuzzy green leaves. Add to the appeal of this newly developed variety of carrot.

2. Living with gusto. That is what many Americans yearn for.

3. The region has dry, sandy soil. Blown into strange formations by the ever-present wind.

4. The climbers had two choices. To go over a four-hundred-foot cliff or to turn back. They decided to make the attempt.

5. Connie picked up the cat and started playing with it. It scratched her neck. With its sharp little claws.

6. The president promoted one tax change. A reduction in the capital gains tax.

7. Trying to carry a portfolio, art box, illustration boards, and drawing pads. I must have looked ridiculous.

8. Organized crime has been able to attract graduates just as big business has. With good pay and the best equipment money can buy.

9. Joan ate her lunch. Then began studying for a midterm.

10. Wollstonecraft believed in universal public education. Also, in education that forms the heart and strengthens the body.

23.2 Revising a paragraph to eliminate sentence fragments

Underline every fragment you find in the following paragraph. Then revise the paragraph. You may combine or rearrange sentences in any way you see fit, as long as you retain the original content. You need not eliminate every single fragment, but if you keep one, identify it, and briefly explain your decision. (See *The Everyday Writer,* pp. 148–152.)

Because water supplies are limited in many areas. We need to conserve water. In as many ways as possible. Most people who have experienced water shortages have learned to take shorter showers. To avoid wasting water doing dishes, and to save water in other ways. When people do not have plentiful water to drink or to use for bathing and washing. They cannot afford to waste water on their lawns and plants. As a result. Water companies, extension offices, and nurseries encourage gardeners to select low-water plants. Adding large borders of low-maintenance, low-water shrubs and plants to a yard. That is almost all grass. Will save water. In fact, water usage may be cut in half. Besides saving water for other uses. Such changes also save money because water bills are lower.

Words/Glossary

24.1 Using formal register

Revise each of the following sentences to use formal register consistently, eliminating colloquial or slang terms. (See *The Everyday Writer,* pp. 155–157.) Example:

> Although be excited   as soon as
> I can ~~get all enthused~~ about writing, ~~but~~ I sit down to write my
> ^   ^ blank.
> mind goes ~~right to sleep.~~
>   ^

1. Desdemona's attitude is that of a wimp; she just lies down and dies, accepting her death as inevitable.

2. All candidates strive for the same results: you try to make the other guy look gross and to persuade voters that you're okay for the job.

3. Often, instead of firing an incompetent teacher, school officials will transfer the person to another school in order to avoid the hassles involved in a dismissal.

4. The more she flipped out about his actions, the more he rebelled and continued doing what he pleased.

5. My family lived in Trinidad for the first ten years of my life, and we went through a lot; but when we came to America, we thought we had it made.

6. Moby Dick's humongous size was matched only by Ahab's obsessive desire to wipe him out.

7. Some grunts in Vietnam were accused of freaking out and wasting inno-cent civilians.

8. This essay will trash Mr. Buckley's goofy argument.

9. Every election year, public-service announcements urge us all to boogie on down to our respective polling places and make our preferences known.

10. James Agee's most famous novel, *A Death in the Family*, focuses on a young boy and on what happens after his old man croaks in a car wreck.

24.2   Checking for correct denotation

Read each of the following sentences, looking for denotative errors, using your dictionary as needed. Underline every error that you find. Then examine each error to determine the word intended, and write in the correct word. If a sentence has no error, write C. (See *The Everyday Writer*, p. 157.) Example:

> conscience
> Your ~~conscious~~ would tell you that dishonesty is not the best policy.
> ^

1. A rabbit's foot or similar talisman gives some people the allusion of security.

2. She is an imminent attorney, highly regarded by her opponents in court as well as by her colleagues.

3. Conscientious employees typically expect promotions and regular increases in compensation.

4. Now that our analyses are complete, you can expect our confidential purport by the end of this month.

5. When emergency personnel arrived, the victim was conscience and alert.

6. Encyclopedias often feature both biographical and geographical entries.

7. Don't let the judges effect the way you feel about yourself.

8. One literary illusion in this poem may be referring to Frost's "After Apple-Picking."

9. Eating squid somehow goes against my native deposition.

10. Bjorn Borg's baseline game was very affective against John McEnroe's style of play.

24.3 Revising sentences to change connotations

The sentences that follow contain words with strongly judgmental connotative meanings. Underline these words; then revise each sentence to make it sound more neutral. (See *The Everyday Writer*, p. 157.) Example:

> The current NRA <u>scheme</u> appeals to patriotism as a <u>smokescreen to obscure the real issue</u> of gun control.
>
> The current NRA campaign appeals to patriotism rather than responding directly to gun-control proposals.

1. News media crackpots claim that their news reports are fair and impartial.

2. Prochoice sympathizers keep screaming that a ban on abortion would drive abortion out of hospitals and into back alleys.

3. A mob of protesters appeared, yelling and jabbing their signs in the air.

4. Liberals keep whining about the bums, the crazies, and the lazy.

5. Only recently have ladies landed a seat on the Supreme Court.

6. Each election year, packs of Republicans swarm together at a national convention, itching to finger a figurehead.

7. Naive voters often stumble to the polls and blithely yank whichever handles are closest to them.

8. The Democrats are conspiring on a new education bill.

24.4 Considering connotation

Study the italicized words in each of the following passages, and decide what each word's connotations contribute to your understanding of the passage. Think of a synonym for each word, and see whether you can decide what difference the new word would make to the effect of the passage. (See *The Everyday Writer*, p. 157.)

1. The Burmans were already *racing* past me across the mud. It was obvious that the elephant would never *rise* again, but he was not dead. He was breathing very rhythmically with long *rattling* gasps, his great *mound* of a side painfully rising and falling.

   – GEORGE ORWELL, "Shooting an Elephant"

2. If boxing is a sport, it is the most *tragic* of all sports because, more than any [other] human activity, it *consumes* the very excellence it *displays:* Its very *drama* is this consumption.

   – JOYCE CAROL OATES, "On Boxing"

3. We caught two bass, *hauling* them in *briskly* as though they were mackerel, pulling them over the side of the boat in a *businesslike* manner without any landing net, and stunning them with a *blow* on the back of the head.

   – E. B. WHITE, "Once More to the Lake"

4. Then one evening Miss Glory told me to serve the ladies on the porch. After I set the tray down and turned toward the kitchen, one of the women asked, "What's your name, *girl*?"
   – MAYA ANGELOU, *I Know Why the Caged Bird Sings*

5. The Kiowas are a summer people; they *abide* the cold and keep to themselves; but when the season *turns* and the land becomes warm and *vital*, they cannot *hold still*.
   – N. SCOTT MOMADAY, "The Way to Rainy Mountain"

24.5 Using specific and concrete words

Rewrite each of the following sentences to be more specific and more concrete. (See *The Everyday Writer*, pp. 158–159.) Example:

The weather this summer has varied.

Going from clear, dry days, on which the breeze seems to scrub the sky, to the so-called dog days of oppressive humidity, July and August have offered two extremes of weather.

1. The entryway of the building was dirty.

2. The sounds at dawn are memorable.

3. Sunday dinner was good.

4. The attendant came toward my car.

5. The child played on the beach.

6. My neighbor is a nuisance.

7. Central Texas has an unusual climate.

8. The president's speech touched on many important topics.

9. One student asked the president a question.

10. The president answered the question.

24.6 Thinking about similes and metaphors

Identify the similes and metaphors in the following numbered items, and decide how each contributes to your understanding of the passage or sentence it appears in. (See *The Everyday Writer*, pp. 159–160.)

1. John's mother, Mom Willie, who wore her Southern background like a magnolia corsage, eternally fresh, was robust and in her sixties.

   – MAYA ANGELOU, "The Heart of a Woman"

2. I was watching everyone else and didn't see the waitress standing quietly by. Her voice was deep and soft like water moving in a cavern.

   – WILLIAM LEAST HEAT MOON, "In the Land of 'Coke-Cola'"

3. My horse, when he is in his stall or lounging about the pasture, has the same relationship to pain that I have when cuddling up with a good murder mystery—comfort and convenience have top priority.

   – VICKI HEARNE, "Horses in Partnership with Time"

4. The fog hangs among the trees like veils of trailing lace.

   – STEPHANIE VAUGHN, "My Mother Breathing Light"

5. The migraine acted as a circuit breaker, and the fuses have emerged intact.

   – JOAN DIDION, "In Bed"

6. Black women are called, in the folklore that so aptly identifies one's status in society, "the mule of the world," because we have been handed the burdens that everyone else—everyone else—refused to carry.

   – ALICE WALKER, *In Search of Our Mothers' Gardens*

7. The lawn cried out for water.

8. Producing broccoli, carrots, lettuce, cucumbers, even corn—the tiny garden was a produce section all by itself.

9. Like huge matchsticks on the horizon, the tinder-dry pines flared one by one as the flames reached them.

10. A whip cracking in the wind, the flag stood out, taut and rippling.

25.1 Identifying stereotypes

Each of the following sentences stereotypes a person or a group of people. Underline the word or phrase that identifies the stereotyped person or group. In each case, be ready to explain why the stereotype may be offensive, demeaning, or unfair. (See *The Everyday Writer,* p. 162.)

1. The ambulance chasers have clogged our court system.

2. When we visit the nursing home, remember to treat each of the old folks with respect.

3. Dropouts have trouble landing good jobs.

4. College kids need real-world experience.

5. Why would blue-collar types care about art?

6. Teenagers are irresponsible.

7. Academics are extremely well paid, considering how few hours they actually teach.

8. Why are those Harvard-educated doctors always belly-aching about insurance?

25.2 Identifying and revising sexist language

The following excerpt is taken from the 1968 edition of Dr. Benjamin Spock's *Baby and Child Care*. Read it carefully, noting any language we might today consider sexist. Then try bringing it up to date by revising the passage, substituting nonsexist language as necessary. (See *The Everyday Writer*, pp. 163–164.)

399. Feeling his oats. One year old is an exciting age. Your baby is changing in lots of ways—in his eating, in how he gets around, in what he wants to do and in how he feels about himself and other people. When he was little and helpless, you could put him where you wanted him, give him the playthings you thought suitable, feed him the foods you knew were best. Most of the time he was willing to let you be the boss, and took it all in good spirit. It's more complicated now that he is around a year old. He seems to realize that he's not meant to be a baby doll the rest of his life, that he's a human being with ideas and a will of his own.

When you suggest something that doesn't appeal to him, he feels he must assert himself. His nature tells him to. He just says No in words or actions, even about things that he likes to do. The psychologists call it "negativism"; mothers call it "that terrible No stage." But stop and think what would happen to him if he never felt like saying No. He'd become a robot, a mechanical man. You wouldn't be able to resist the temptation to boss him all the time, and he'd stop learning and developing. When he was old enough to go out into the world, to school and later to work, everybody else would take advantage of him, too. He'd never be good for anything.

25.3 Rewriting to eliminate offensive references

Review the following sentences for offensive references or terms. If a sentence seems acceptable as written, write *C*. If a sentence contains unacceptable terms, rewrite it. (See *The Everyday Writer*, pp. 165–167.) Example:

> Passengers
> ~~Elderly~~ ~~passengers~~ on the cruise ship *Romance Afloat* will enjoy
> ^
> swimming, shuffleboard, and nightly movies.

1. Blind psychology professor Dr. Charles Warnath gave the keynote address last night.

2. Our skylight was installed last week by a woman carpenter.

3. Seventy-six-year-old Jewish violinist Josh Mickle, last night's featured soloist, brought the crowd to its feet.

4. These days a secretary has to know her word-processing skills.

5. Despite the plane's mechanical problems, the crewmen were able to calm the passengers and land safely.

6. People like mill workers probably don't listen to the classical music station.

7. Each home economics student should be proud of the courses she takes.

8. African American actor Denzel Washington appeared at a charity benefit last night.

9. A West Point cadet must keep his record clean if he expects to excel in his chosen career.

10. Acting as a spokesman and speaking with a southern twang, Cynthia McDowell, attractive mother of two, vowed that all elementary school-teachers in the district would take their turns on the picket line until the school board agreed to resume negotiations.

27.1 Recognizing correct spellings

Choose the correct spelling from the pair of words in the parentheses in each of the following sentences. (See *The Everyday Writer*, pp. 173–179.) Example:

> The plane to Chicago (<u>may be</u>/maybe) late; (<u>therefore</u>/therfore), we
>
> don't need to leave for the airport (imediately/<u>immediately</u>).

1. (Their/There/They're) going to put (their/there/they're) new stereo system over (their/there/they're) in the corner.

2. My little brother wants (to/too) go swimming, (to/too).

3. The (begining/beginning) of school is (a lot/alot) earlier this year than last.

4. The rise in temperature isn't (noticable/noticeable) (until/untill) the humidity rises.

5. The accident (occured/occurred) (before/befour) I could step aside.

6. We couldn't (beleive/believe) the national champions were expected to (loose/lose) the play-offs.

7. In making your major life decisions, (your/you're) (definately/definitely) on (your/you're) own.

8. Nothing (affects/effects) (success/sucess) more (than/then) self-confidence or (its/it's) absence.

9. We (received/recieved) our notice (threw/through) the mail.

10. The group hopes to (develop/develope) a (truely/truly) (succesful/successful) fast-food franchise.

11. We (can not/cannot) easily (separate/seperate) fact and opinion.

12. Please tell me (wear/where) (an/and) when we should meet.

13. Our (argumants/arguments) (against/aginst) continuing to pollute the (enviroment/environment) fell on deaf ears.

14. Local (busineses/businesses) are (dependant/dependent) on the summer tourist trade.

15. (Heroes/Heros) are (necesary/necessary) to every culture's mythology.

16. Our first (experiance/experience) with aerobic (exercise/exercize) left us tired.

17. The (professor/profesor) agreed to (accept/except) our final research essays on Friday.

18. She qualified for three (catagories/categories) in the (final/finel) gymnastics competition.

19. The two (roomates/roommates) would be lost (without/witout) each other.

20. We intend to celebrate the (ocasion/occasion) (weather/whether) or not the (weather/whether) cooperates.

27.2 Distinguishing between homonyms

Choose the appropriate word in each pair of parentheses. (See *The Everyday Writer*, pp. 174–177.) Example:

Don't (<u>accept</u>/except) any substitutes.

If (your/you're) looking for summer fun, (accept/except) the friendly (advice/advise) of thousands of happy adventurers: spend three (weaks/weeks) kayaking (threw/thorough/through) the inside passage (to/too/two) Alaska. For ten years, Outings, Inc., has (lead/led) groups of novice kayakers (passed/past) some of the most breathtaking scenery in North America. (Their/There/They're) goal is simple: to give participants the time of (their/there/they're) lives. As one of last year's adventurers said, "(Its/It's) a trip I will remember vividly, one that (affected/effected) me powerfully."

27.3 Spelling plurals

Form the plural of each of the following words. (See *The Everyday Writer*, p. 179.) Example:

fox foxes

1. tomato

2. mother-in-law

3. volunteer

4. baby

5. dish

6. radio

7. beach

8. phenomenon

9. golf club

10. rose

11. stepchild

12. turkey

28.1 Selecting the appropriate word

Choose the appropriate word for each of the following sentences from the pair of words in parentheses. (See *The Everyday Writer,* pp. 180–190.) Example:

She looked fragile and (<u>weak</u>/week).

1. Many young people are missing (a/an) historical perspective.

2. The hikers decided to rest in (a while/awhile).

3. She annoyed the host by not immediately (accepting/excepting) the invitation.

4. He feels (bad/badly) that he hurt my feelings.

5. No one (beside/besides) my younger brother wants to go to the circus.

6. For each of the following pairs, choose the appropriate term; that is, choose (among/between) *bring* and *take, can* and *may,* and *borrow* and *lend.*

7. I burned off (fewer/less) calories than I'd hoped to.

8. We hiked (farther/further) than we had intended.

9. Debate persists over whether criminals on death row should be (hanged/hung).

10. Please say (if/whether) you like my haircut.

11. The mediocre food tasted great (as/like) mediocre food tends to after a fast.

12. The calm (preceded/proceeded) the storm.

13. Answer the judge clearly and (respectfully/respectively).

14. The ticket to the concert was considerably more expensive (than/then) I'd hoped it would be.

15. The three (principals/principles) in the company couldn't agree among themselves.

16. Set off the (quotation/quote) with the appropriate punctuation.

17. When he (raises/rises) his glass in a toast, be polite enough to stand up.

18. The (reason/reason why) she didn't win the race should be self-evident.

19. The bus was (stationary/stationery) for at least an hour.

20. If the two of them can't reach an agreement, they're going to have to call in a (disinterested/uninterested) party.

28.2 Editing inappropriate words

In each of the following sentences, remove or replace inappropriate words. If all the words in a sentence are appropriate, mark the sentence C. (See *The Everyday Writer*, pp. 180–190.) Example:

> *can*
> The pilot ~~can't~~ hardly see in such a fog.
>   ^

1. Fifty states comprise the United States.

2. The artist created a new affect by dribbling paint on the canvas.

3. To charm parents or friends, bring them five miles down the road to the new restaurant.

4. The rich cream complements the figs.

5. If they are holding out for a consensus of opinion, they are going to have a long wait.

6. The principal could of been more encouraging when talking to the parents.

7. If the data was corrupt, the experiment was worthless.

8. Leave the child a chance to figure out the puzzle on her own.

9. When I loose weight, my clothes become loose.

10. I was good and ready for the final exam.

11. Hopefully, it won't rain during the company outing.

12. Its never a waste of time to check each instance of *its* and *it's* to be sure you've used the right homonym.

13. The temperature is so high that one could literally cook dinner on the sidewalk.

14. She emigrated to New York in the 1920s.

15. Swiss cheese is different than Jarlsberg.

16. A small percent of the graduates weren't qualified for the entry-level positions.

17. After gathering the chemicals and the instruments, you can proceed with the experiment.

18. The supervisor and trainee speak to each other everyday.

19. The supervisor tries not to flaunt the trainee's confusion with the computer program.

20. When he finally mastered the program, the trainee had a tendency to flaunt his newly acquired talent.

Punctuation/Mechanics

29.1   Using a comma to set off introductory elements

In the following sentences, add any commas that are needed after the introductory element. If no comma is necessary, write C. (See *The Everyday Writer*, p. 195.) Example:

> **To reduce the heat in the room, draw the shades or curtains.**
>   ^

1. In one of his most famous poems Frost asks why people need walls.

2. Unfortunately the door to the kennel had been left open.

3. Unable to make such a decision alone I asked my brother for help.

4. If you follow the instructions you will be able to install your radio.

5. Therefore answering the seemingly simple question is very difficult.

6. With the fifth century came the fall of the Roman Empire.

7. Their bags packed they waited for the taxi to the airport.

8. To become an Olympic competitor an athlete must train for years.

9. After the hurricane moved on the citizens of the town assessed the damage.

10. Startled by the explosion the workers dropped to the ground.

29.2   Using a comma in compound sentences

Use a comma and a coordinating conjunction (*and, but, or, for, nor, so,* or *yet*) to combine each of the following pairs of sentences into one sentence. Delete or rearrange words if necessary. (See *The Everyday Writer,* pp. 195–196.) Example:

I had finished studying for the test / I went to bed. , so

1. Max Weber was not in favor of a classless society. He thought it would lead to the expansion of the power of the state over the individual.

2. Joan Didion's nonfiction is renowned. Her novels are also worthwhile.

3. I have studied ten of Verdi's operas. I have only begun to appreciate the wealth of his creativity.

4. The playwright disliked arguing with directors. She avoided rehearsals.

5. Tropical fish do not bark. They are not cuddly pets.

6. The sun shone. The sky was a clear, deep blue.

7. Yesterday was hot and steamy. Today a cool wind has made the apartment more comfortable.

8. The geography final had me worried. I studied for two hours after lunch.

9. The sprinkler had been running for forty-five minutes. The water has penetrated only an inch.

10. She could not keep her eyes open. She had been up al! night.

29.3 Recognizing restrictive and nonrestrictive elements

First, underline the restrictive or the nonrestrictive elements in the following sentences. Then, use commas to set off the nonrestrictive elements in any of the sentences that contain such elements. (See *The Everyday Writer*, pp. 196–199.) Example:

My only novel, *The Family Kurasch*, is out of print.

1. The tornado which had spared Waterville leveled Douglastown.

2. The man who rescued her puppy won her eternal gratitude.

3. Jacqueline Kennedy Onassis who died in 1994 was a figure of mystery.

4. Houses made of wood can often survive earthquakes.

5. Thurgood Marshall the first African American to serve on the U.S. Supreme Court died in 1993.

6. Anyone who is fourteen years old faces strong peer pressure every day.

7. Embalming is a technique that preserves a cadaver.

8. I would feel right at home in the city dump which bears a striking resemblance to my bedroom.

9. The musical *West Side Story* is a modern version of Shakespeare's play *Romeo and Juliet*.

10. A house overlooking the ocean costs $500,000.

11. The Zuñis an ancient tribe live in New Mexico.

12. The president elected for a six-year term acts as head of state.

13. Karl Marx an important nineteenth-century political philosopher believed that his role as a social thinker was to change the world.

14. Birds' hearts have four chambers whereas reptiles' have three.

15. Britain and France agreed to aid each other if one of them were attacked.

29.4 Using commas to set off items in a series

In the following sentences, add any commas that are needed to set off words, phrases, or clauses in a series. If no comma is needed, write C. (See *The Everyday Writer,* p. 199.) Example:

The waiter brought water, menus, and an attitude.
$\qquad$ ^ $\qquad$ ^

1. They found employment in truck driving farming and mining.

2. We bought zucchini peppers and tomatoes at the market.

3. James Joyce wrote novels short stories and poems.

4. The spider's orange body resembles a colored dot amidst eight long black legs.

5. The blackberry pie smelled delicious looked absolutely inviting and tasted divine.

6. Superficial observation does not provide accurate insight into people's lives—how they feel what they believe in how they respond to others.

7. The ball sailed over the fence across the road and through the Wilsons' window.

8. I timidly offered to help a loud overbearing lavishly dressed customer.

9. Ellen is an accomplished freelance writer.

10. The moon circles the earth the earth revolves around the sun and the sun is just one star among many in the Milky Way galaxy.

29.5 Using commas to set off parenthetical and transitional expressions, contrasting elements, interjections, direct address, and tag questions

Revise each of the following sentences, using commas to set off parenthetical and transitional expressions, contrasting elements, interjections, words used in direct address, and tag questions. (See *The Everyday Writer*, p. 200.)

> **Ladies and gentlemen, thank you for your attention.**
>   ^

1. One must consider the society as a whole not just its parts.

2. The West in fact has become solidly Republican in presidential elections.

3. Her friends did not know about her illness did they?

4. Ladies and gentlemen I bid you farewell.

5. The celebration will alas conclude all too soon.

6. Hey stop ogling that construction worker!

7. Last year I am sorry to say six elms had to be destroyed.

8. "Bill could you read over the third paragraph?"

9. Now we can stitch the seam right?

10. Joey enjoys chocolate milkshakes but only those made with vanilla ice cream.

29.6 Using commas with dates, addresses, titles, numbers, and quotations

Revise each of the following sentences, using commas appropriately with dates, addresses and place-names, titles, numbers, and quotations. If no comma is needed in a sentence, write *C*. (See *The Everyday Writer*, pp. 201–202.) Example:

The wine store's original location was 2373 Broadway, New York City.
                                                                    ^

1. In my dictionary, the rules of punctuation begin on page 1560.

2. Ithaca New York has a population of about 30000.

3. The ship was hit by two torpedoes on May 7 1915 and sank in minutes.

4. MLA headquarters are at 10 Astor Place New York New York 10003.

5. The nameplate read *Donald Good R.N.* and looked quite impressive.

6. "The public be damned!" William Henry Vanderbilt was reported to have said. "I'm working for my stockholders."

7. Joseph Epstein admits "I prefer not to be thought vulgar in any wise."

8. Who remarked that "youth is wasted on the young"?

9. "Neat people are lazier and meaner than sloppy people" according to Suzanne Britt.

10. "Who shall decide when doctors disagree?" asked Alexander Pope.

29.7 Eliminating unnecessary and inappropriate commas

Revise each of the following sentences, deleting unnecessary commas. (See *The Everyday Writer*, pp. 203–204.) Example:

The child wanted/ red, yellow, and blue/ balloons.

1. The four types of nonverbal communication are, kinesic, haptic, proxemic, and dormant, communication.

2. Observers watch facial expressions and gestures, and interpret them.

3. We could see nothing, except jagged peaks, for miles around.

4. Our supper that evening, consisted of stale bologna sandwiches.

5. Clothes, that had to be ironed, were too much trouble.

6. Sitting around the campfire, we felt boredom, and disappointment.

7. Magazines, like *Modern Maturity,* are aimed at retired people.

8. The photographer, Edward Curtis, is known for his depiction of the West.

9. We all took panicked, hasty, looks at our notebooks.

10. Driving a car, and talking on the car phone at the same time demand care.

30.1   Using semicolons to link clauses

Combine each of the following pairs of sentences into one sentence by using a semicolon. (See *The Everyday Writer,* pp. 204–206.) Example:

$; meet$
Take the bus to Henderson Street, ~~Meet~~ me under the clock.

1. Establishing your position in an office is an important task. Your profile will mold your relationships with other staff members.

2. City life offers many advantages. In many ways, however, life in a small town is much more pleasant.

3. Florida's mild winter climate is ideal for bicycling. In addition, the terrain is very flat.

4. Physical education forms an important part of a university's program. Nevertheless, few students and professors clearly recognize its value.

5. The debate over political correctness affects more than the curriculum. It also affects students' social relationships.

6. Voltaire was concerned about the political implications of his skepticism. He warned his friends not to discuss atheism in front of the servants.

7. The unwanted package arrived C.O.D. I politely refused to pay the charges.

8. My high school was excessively competitive. Virtually everyone went on to college, many to the top schools in the nation.

9. Pittsburgh was once notorious for its smoke and grime. Today, its skies and streets are cleaner than those of many other American cities.

10. *Propaganda* is defined as the spread of ideas to further a cause. Therefore, *propaganda* and *advertisement* are synonyms.

30.2 Eliminating misused semicolons

Revise each of the following sentences to correct the misuse of semicolons. (See *The Everyday Writer*, p. 207.) Example:

The new system would encourage high school students to take more academic courses⁄‚ thus strengthening college preparation.

1. We accept the following forms of payment; cash, check, money order, or credit card.

2. If the North had followed up its victory at Gettysburg more vigorously; the Civil War might have ended sooner.

3. He left a large estate; which was used to endow a scholarship fund.

4. We must find a plan to provide decent health care; a necessity in today's life.

5. Verbal scores have decreased more than fifty-four points; while math scores have decreased more than thirty-six.

6. For four glorious but underpaid weeks; I'll be working in Yosemite this summer.

7. Swinging the door open quietly; the two police officers surprised a young burglar as he worked; to disconnect the cable wire from the Tuckers' television.

8. My current work-study job ends in two weeks. I'll need to find a new position; starting next term.

9. Please save your questions for the end of the presentation; if you don't understand.

10. Some gardeners want; low-maintenance plants, limited grass to mow, and low water usage.

31.1   Using periods appropriately

Revise each of the following items, inserting periods in the appropriate places and eliminating any inappropriate punctuation. (See *The Everyday Writer*, pp. 207–208.) Example:

Ms. Maria Jordan received both a Ph.D. in chemistry and an M.Ed.

1. Please attend the meeting on Tuesday at 10:00 AM in Room 401.

2. Cicero was murdered in 43 BC

3. "Have you lost something, Charles?" I inquired

4. She asked whether the operation had been founded by Jesse Jackson

5. A voluntary effort by doctors could help contain hospital costs

6. I just asked you what time it was?

7. Dr Noland and Mr Weber are in conference.

8. Write the check to Richard Steins, M.D..

9. "Halt!" yelled the border guard!

10. Please change the record, then come sit down.

31.2 Using question marks appropriately

Revise each of the following sentences, adding question marks, substituting question marks for other punctuation where appropriate, and removing inappropriately placed question marks. Some sentences do not require any question marks. (See *The Everyday Writer*, pp. 208–209.) Example:

She asked the travel agent, "What is the air fare to Greece ⸮/"

1. Social scientists face difficult questions: should they use their knowl-

   edge to shape society, merely describe human behavior, try to do both.

2. What do you think of your new office? your new salary?

3. "Can I play this" asked Manuel.

4. I looked at him and asked what his point was.

5. The judge asked, "What is your verdict."

6. Who said, "Give me liberty, or give me death?"

7. Didn't I say? "Either clean up your room , or there'll be no desserts after

   dinner"?

8. "Have you heard the one about the tourist and the barber," he asked.

9. Did you just say, "What time is it?"?

10. Learning how to be a curious traveler is a good way to find out about U.S. history?

31.3   Using exclamation points appropriately

Revise each of the following sentences, adding or deleting exclamation points as necessary and removing any other inappropriate punctuation that you find. (See *The Everyday Writer*, p. 209.) Example:

$$! \text{ The}$$
Look out/ the tide is coming in fast/ !

1. She exclaimed, "It's too hot."

2. I screamed at Jamie, "You rat. You tricked me."

3. "This time we're starting early!," she shouted.

4. Stop, thief.

5. Oh, no. We've lost the house.

6. What, exactly, do you want!?

7. "What a riot," she shouted!

8. The only thing the surprised guest of honor could say was, "Well, I'll be!".

9. It was an ordinary school day, so the child once again came home to an empty house!

10. The child cried, "Ouch" as her mother pulled off the bandage!

32.1 Using apostrophes to signal possession

Complete each of the following sentences by inserting *'s* or an apostrophe alone to form the possessive case of the italicized words. (See *The Everyday Writer,* pp. 210–211.) Example:

The blackout was the Internet *provider*'s worst nightmare.

1. Grammar is *everybody* favorite subject.

2. *Maria Callas* opera performances are now the stuff of legend.

3. I was having a good time at *P.J.,* but my friends wanted to go to *Barbara.*

4. *Carol and Jim* combined income dropped drastically after Jim lost his job.

5. Parents often question their *children* choice of friends.

6. Many smokers disregard the *surgeon general* warnings.

7. How the economy will recover is *anyone* guess.

8. The *governors* attitudes changed after the convention.

9. This dog has a *beagle* ears and a *St. Bernard* nose and feet.

10. *My friend and my brother* cars have the same kind of stereo system.

32.2 Using apostrophes to create contractions

Revise each of the following sentences so that it uses contractions. Remove any misused apostrophes. (See *The Everyday Writer,* p. 212.) Example:

~~That is~~ That's the classical music used in the movie *Elvira Madigan.*

1. Should not we have stopped at Dairy Mart for more milk?

2. You have been listening to several folks as they have described how the

United Way has helped them; now will you not please take out your checkbooks and help your neighbors?

3. That fellow who has been giving you a ride after work called at about nine o'clock.

4. Who will the critics identify as the best new novelist of the decade?

5. The clothes I am washing now did not really get too dirty.

6. For the test you will be taking on Monday, you are required to have a pencil with No. 2 lead.

7. The distributor says that your order has not received it's approval from the business office.

8. Who is responsible for that accident?

9. Is not that the new jazz club that is open on weekends?

10. It is true that a snake can shed it's own skin and can swallow much of it's prey whole.

33.1 Using quotation marks to signal direct quotations

In the following sentences, add quotation marks each time someone else's exact words are being used. Some sentences do not require quotation marks. (See *The Everyday Writer*, pp. 213–214.) Example:

"Your phone's ringing!" yelled Phil from the end of the hall.

1. Ultimately, our differences with management may result in the need to strike. The crowd shifted uneasily at those words.

2. I'm going outside for some fresh air, said Ryan, but I'll only be a few minutes.

3. We all heard Mrs. Fleming say, For the duration of these training seminars, we will not tolerate absences.

4. I could not believe the condition of my hometown, he wrote.

5. The nineteenth-century writer Ralph Waldo Emerson said, A foolish consistency is the hobgoblin of little minds.

6. After a tornado ripped through her house, a tearful Indiana woman said she had nothing left.

7. Call me Ishmael is the first sentence of novelist Herman Melville's *Moby Dick.*

8. Most people like to think of themselves as open-minded and flexible enough to change when the circumstances demand.

9. The county employment office's annual summary states that the current unemployment rate is 37 percent lower than it was five years ago.

10. To repeat their words, the worst is behind us.

33.2 Using quotation marks for definitions and titles

Revise each of the following sentences, using quotation marks appropriately to signal titles and definitions. (See *The Everyday Writer,* p. 215.) Example:

The Chinese American businessman surprised his guest by using the Hebrew word *shalom*, which means "peace."

1. Kowinski uses the term *mallaise* to mean physical and psychological disturbances caused by mall contact.

2. In Flannery O'Connor's short story Revelation, colors symbolize passion, violence, sadness, and even God.

3. "The little that is known about gorillas certainly makes you want to know more," writes Alan Moorehead in his essay A Most Forgiving Ape.

4. The British, the guide told us, knit sweaters for their teapots.

5. Wolfe's article Radical Chic satirizes wealthy liberals.

6. Big Bill, a section of Dos Passos's book *U.S.A.*, opens with a birth.

7. Amy Lowell challenges social conformity in her poem Patterns.

8. The song Love Me Do catapulted the Beatles to international stardom.

9. My dictionary defines *isolation* as the quality or state of being alone.

10. In the episode Driven to Extremes, *48 Hours* takes a humorous look at driving in New York City.

33.3 Using quotation marks appropriately

Revise each of the following sentences, deleting quotation marks used inappropriately and moving those placed incorrectly. (See *The Everyday Writer,* pp. 213–217.) Example:

In "Bartleby the Scrivener",Bartleby states time and again, "I would prefer not to".

1. The grandmother in O'Connor's story shows she is still misguided when she says, "You've got good blood! I know you wouldn't shoot a lady"!

2. What is Hawthorne telling the readers in "Rappaccini's Daughter?"

3. Very quietly, Chun Lee said, "I know the answer".

4. 'Buddhist Economics' is not a chapter title you'll find in too many college textbooks.

5. Being "overweight" is a problem because "excess pounds" are hard to lose and can be "dangerous" to a person's health.

6. One of Joyce Carol Oates's most shocking stories is "Bingo Master;" in it, the triumph of brutality is devastating.

7. Macbeth "bumps off" Duncan to gain the throne for himself.

8. In his article "The Death of Broadway", Thomas M. Disch writes that "choreographers are, literally, a dying breed[1]".

9. "Know thyself:" this is the quest of the main characters in both Ibsen's *Peer Gynt* and Lewis's *Till We Have Faces*.

10. One thought flashed through my mind as I finished the book "*In Search of Our Mothers' Gardens:*" I want to read more of this writer's books.

34.1 Using parentheses and brackets

Revise the following sentences, using parentheses and brackets correctly. (See *The Everyday Writer*, pp. 218–220.) Example:

She was in fourth grade (or was it third?) when she became blind.

1. One incident of cruelty was brought to public attention by the Animal Liberation Front ALF.

2. During my research, I found that a flat-rate income tax a single-rate tax with no deductions has its problems.

3. The health-care expert informed readers that "as we progress through middle age, we experience intimations of our own morality *sic*."

4. Many researchers used the Massachusetts Multiphasic Personality Inventory the MMPI for hypnotizability studies.

5. Some of the alternatives suggested include 1 tissue cultures, 2 mechanical models, 3 in vitro techniques, and 4 mathematical and electrical models.

6. That mantel clock made in Germany in 1888 has been in the family since my father's grandmother brought it over with her in 1901.

7. "Her book *Out of Africa* is to me both an astonishment and a delight." [Assume that the title of the book has been inserted and was not part of the original quoted sentence.]

8. The Republican party has not always been unsympathetic to feminist concerns (such as the Equal Rights Amendment ERA, which the Nixon administration supported).

9. Walt Disney's movie *Alice in Wonderland* 1951 remains a bright, weird tale even on television's small screen.

10. Then she turned and said, "Will you meaning my father be joining us for dinner?"

34.2 Using dashes

Punctuate the following sentences with dashes where appropriate. (See *The Everyday Writer,* p. 220–221.) Example:

He is quick, violent, and mean they don't call him Dirty Harry for nothing but appealing nonetheless.

1. Many people would have ignored the children's taunts but not Ace.

2. Even if smoking is harmful and there is no real proof of this assertion it is unjust to outlaw smoking while other harmful substances remain legal.

3. Saving old theaters how many have we already lost? is a cultural necessity.

4. Union Carbide's plant in Bhopal, India, sprang a leak a leak that killed more than 2,000 people and injured an additional 200,000.

5. Fair-skinned people and especially those with red hair should use a strong sunscreen.

6. "I wait *no* don't shoot I'll tell you what you want to know."

7. Dorothy Hamill was a joy to watch on the ice graceful, athletic, intense.

8. We'll meet you at nine at Woodstock's for pizza if Rob's aging Buick can get there.

9. As a boy, I lived next door to John Glenn the former astronaut who was later a U.S. senator and mowed his lawn every Saturday.

10. Several kinds of lace among them Alencon, Honiton, and Maltese take their names from their place of origin.

34.3 Using colons

Insert a colon in each of the following items that needs one. Some of the items do not require a colon. (See *The Everyday Writer,* pp. 221–223.) Example:

> *Images*: *My Life in Film* includes revealing material written by
> ^
> **Ingmar Bergman.**

1. The sonnet's structure is effective in revealing the speaker's message love has changed his life and ended his depression.

2. Another example is taken from Psalm 139 16.

3. Reviewers agree that Lisa's book possesses these traits readability, intelligence, and usefulness.

4. Shifting into German, Kennedy declared "Ich bin ein Berliner."

5. Education can alleviate problems such as poverty, poor health, and the energy shortage.

6. Gandhi urged four rules tell the truth even in business, adopt more sanitary habits, abolish caste and religious divisions, and learn English.

7. Solid vocal technique is founded on the correct use of head position, diaphragm control, muscle relaxation, and voice placement.

8. *Signs of Trouble and Erosion A Report on Education in America* was submitted to Congress and the president in January 1984.

9. Even more important was what money represented success, prestige, and power.

10. Two buses go to Denver one at 9 38 A.M. and one at 2 55 P.M.

34.4 Using ellipses

Read the following passage. Then assume that the underlined portions have been left out in a reprinting of the passage. Indicate how you would use ellipses to indicate those deletions. (See *The Everyday Writer*, pp. 223–224.)

Not all states allow the public to remove elected officials from office by recalling them. The fifteen states that do provide for recall have different requirements. They have their own formulas for determining the required number of signatures to be collected. If the formula is based on the number voting in the last election for the office involved, the number of signatures could vary considerably depending on the intensity of the contests that year or the other offices on the ballot. Simply filing the required number of valid signatures might in itself be sufficient to require a recall election. On the other hand, the petitions might need to spell out specific grounds that would justify a recall election. Other differences might occur in registration procedures for petition carriers, signature requirements, and so forth; similar variations might exist in filing deadlines, petition formats, and other details.

34.5 Reviewing punctuation marks

Correct the punctuation in the following sentences. If the punctuation is already correct, write C. (See *The Everyday Writer,* pp. 194–225.) Example:

> **By the time we reached Geneva , we had been traveling more than seven weeks it seemed like seven months! and we were getting rather tired of one another's company.**

1. Even though all of their friends thought Susan and Adam shared much they did not like each other in the slightest.

2. Gina, who is my father's cousin lives in Florence.

3. The china was, totally ruined in the dishwasher.

4. The poems of Wallace Stevens are difficult at first, however, upon further reading their greatness becomes evident.

5. The restaurant advertised for all sorts of workers; short-order cook, busboys, waiters, and bartenders.

6. Whereas Bartholomew kept calling the library a "bookhouse;" I referred to it as "the house of naps."

7. Can working with a computer really improve one's writing," they asked.

8. When I read the judges decision, I decided that they had not paid sufficient attention to the defenses arguments.

9. Mother does not care what the critics say; she just doesnt want to see that movie.

10. The dog kept a close watch on anyone who went near its supper dish.

11. I did not know that this bicycle was their's.

12. I did not know that Ann was coming with us this evening, Peter said.

13. "Eileen said that her job was "very taxing,"" Vincent reported.

14. "Cold and windy,' the weather report said.

15. The police officer said that the robbers 'are now in custody.'

16. In her poem "Crusoe in England," Elizabeth Bishop retells Defoe's novel.

17. A very wise person once said that there are only two types of literature; good and bad.

18. *Where in the World Is Carmen Sandiego?* an ever-popular and hard-to-stock game program has just arrived on our shelves.

19. The invitation distinctly said R.S.V.P., even so, we lost the invitation and never properly responded.

20. Stock analysts refer to IBM International Business Machines as a blue-chip stock.

35.1 Capitalizing

Capitalize words as needed in the following sentences. (See *The Everyday Writer,* pp. 225–229.) Example:

> T S E   T W L   F
> ⱦ. ⱬ. ȼliot, who wrote ⱦhe ᵼaste ȷand, was an editor at ⱦaber
> F
> and ⱦaber.

1. the town in the American south where i was raised had a statue of a civil war soldier in the center of main street.

2. we had a choice of fast-food, chinese, or italian restaurants.

3. I caught a glimpse of president bill clinton and his family.

4. the council of trent was convened to draw up the catholic response to the protestant reformation.

5. We drove east over the hudson river on the tappan zee bridge.

6. i wondered if my new levi's were faded enough.

7. accepting an award for his score for the film *the high and the mighty,* dmitri tiomkin thanked beethoven, brahms, wagner, and strauss.

8. i will cite the novels of vladimir nabokov, in particular *pnin* and *lolita.*

9. the battle of lexington and concord was fought in april 1775.

10. my favorite song by cole porter is "you'd be so nice to come home to."

36.1   Using abbreviations

Revise each of the following sentences to eliminate any abbreviations that would be inappropriate in academic writing. (See *The Everyday Writer,* pp. 229–234.) Example:

United States   percent

The population of the U.S. grew about 10% in the 1980s.

1. The old NBC show is set in a fictional L.A. law firm.

2. An MX missile, which is 71 ft. long and 92 in. around, weighs 190,000 lbs.

3. The waiters prefer the A.M. shift because customers usually order just coffee, tea, doughnuts, etc.

4. In 1991, Rep. William Gray became pres. of the United Negro College Fund.

5. A large corp. like AT&T may help finance an employee's M.B.A.

6. Unfortunately, the five-¢ candy bar is a relic of the past.

7. The preface to the 1851 ed. of *Twice-Told Tales* states that the stories are not autobiographical.

8. The local radio station has a broadcast range of seventy-five mi.

9. After less than a yr. at U.Va., Poe left and joined the U.S. Army.

10. Dostoyevsky was influenced by many European writers—e.g., Dickens, Stendhal, and Balzac.

36.2 Spelling out numbers and using figures

Revise the numbers in the following sentences as necessary for correctness and consistency. If a sentence is correct, write C. (See *The Everyday Writer*, pp. 233–234.) Example:

> twenty-first
> **Does the 21st century begin in 2000 or 2001?**
>   ^

1. 307 miles long and 82 miles wide, the island offered little of interest.

2. Time will provide perspective on the economic crisis of the '80s.

3. You could travel around the city for only 65 cents.

4. The invasion of Kuwait began on August second, 1990.

5. The department received 1,633 calls and forty-three letters.

6. Cable TV is now available to seventy-two percent of the population.

7. Walker signed a three-year, $4.5-million contract.

8. In the 35-to-44 age group, the risk is estimated to be about 1 in 2,500.

9. The parents considered twenty-five cents enough of an allowance for a five-year-old.

10. The amulet measured one and one-eighth by two and two-fifths inches.

37.1 Using italics

In each of the following sentences, underline any words that should be italicized, and circle any italicized words that should not be. (See *The Everyday Writer*, pp. 234–236.) Example:

> **In the essay** (*Is It, or Isn't It?*) **critics debate whether** <u>Thelma & Louise</u> **is a feminist film.**

1. Hawthorne's story *My Kinsman, Major Molineux* bears a striking resemblance to Shakespeare's play A Midsummer Night's Dream.

2. Is Samuel Beckett's play Endgame a sequel to Shakespeare's King Lear?

3. Georgetown offers a *potpourri* of cultures and styles.

4. The word veterinary comes from the Latin *veterinarius*.

5. Niko Tinbergen's essay *The Bee-Hunters of Hulshorst* is a diary of experiments on *Philanthus triangulum Fabr,* the *bee-killer wasp.*

6. Flying the Glamorous Glennis, named for his wife, Chuck Yeager was the first pilot to fly faster than the speed of sound.

7. The Washington Post provides extensive coverage of Congress.

8. The Waste Land is a long and difficult but ultimately rewarding poem.

9. If you have seen only a reproduction of Picasso's Guernica, you can scarcely imagine the impact of the original painting.

10. The White Star liner Titanic sank in the North Atlantic in 1912.

38.1 Using hyphens in compounds and with prefixes

Insert hyphens as needed. A dictionary will help you with some items. If an item does not require a hyphen, write C. (See *The Everyday Writer*, pp. 237–238.) Example:

full-bodied wine

1. deescalate

2. pre World War II

3. pre and post-Wall Berlin

4. happily married couple

5. a what me worry look

6. self important

7. president elect

8. thirty three

9. a hard working farmer

10. a politician who is fast talking

38.2 Using hyphens appropriately

Insert or delete hyphens as necessary, and revise any incorrect word divisions in the following sentences. Use your dictionary if necessary. If a sentence is correct as printed, write C. (See *The Everyday Writer,* pp. 236–238.) Example:

The bleary̅ eyed student finally ⟨stop⟩

/**ped fighting sleep and went to bed.**

1. Stress can lead to hypertension and ulcers.

2. The drum-beating and hand-clapping signaled that the parade was near.

3. The carpenter asked for a two pound bag of three quarter inch nails.

4. Suicide among teen-agers has tripled in the past thirty five years.

5. We urged him to be open minded and to temper his insensitive views.

6. Both pro and antiState Department groups registered complaints.

7. One of Baryshnikov's favorite dancers was none other than Fred A-staire.

8. In Bizet's *Carmen,* the ill-fated Carmen is betrayed by her fic-kleness.

9. The governor elect joked about the preelection polls.

10. The beautifully-written essay earned high praise.

For Multilingual Writers

55.1 Identifying count and noncount nouns

Identify each of the common nouns in the following short paragraph as either a count or a noncount noun. (See *The Everyday Writer,* pp. 391–392.)

In his book *Hiroshima,* John Hersey tells the story of six people who survived the destruction of Hiroshima on August 6, 1945. The bomb detonated at 8:15 in the morning. When the explosion occurred, Mrs. Hatsuyo Nakamura was looking out her window and watching a neighbor work on his house. The force of the explosion lifted her into the air and carried her into the next room, where she was buried by roofing tiles and other debris. When she crawled out, she heard her daughter, Myeko, calling out; she was buried up to her waist and could not move.

55.2 Using appropriate determiners; stating plural forms explicitly

Each of the following sentences contains an error with a noun phrase. Revise each sentence. (See *The Everyday Writer,* pp. 392–393.) Example:

They made a̲ important linguistic breakthrough.
(an)

1. At an end of the eighteenth century, England and France were at war.

2. Napoleon, the French ruler, invaded Egypt with much soldiers.

3. His ultimate goal was India, which England had conquered many year before.

4. At Rosetta, near the Nile, some French soldiers were building fort.

5. They made an historic discovery—the Rosetta Stone.

6. The stone contained three sections of writing.

7. To linguists, the Rosetta Stone became very important.

8. The stone became the basis for an huge insight into ancient writing.

9. Do archeologists think much discoveries like the Rosetta Stone will occur in the future?

10. We do not know what future dig will uncover.

55.3 Using articles appropriately

Insert articles as necessary in the following passage from *The Silent Language,* by Edward T. Hall. If no article is needed, leave the space blank. (See *The Everyday Writer,* pp. 393–395.)

Hollywood is famous for hiring _____ various experts to teach

_____ people technically what most of us learn informally. _____

case in point is _____ story about _____ children of one movie cou-

ple who noticed _____ new child in _____ neighborhood climbing

_____ tree. _____ children immediately wanted to be given

_____ name of his instructor in _____ tree climbing.

55.4 Positioning modifiers

Possible modifiers for each of the following nouns are listed alpha-betically in brackets after the noun. Indicate the order in which the adjectives should precede the noun. (See *The Everyday Writer*, pp. 395–396.) Example:

<u>Popular New Orleans jazz</u> **album (jazz/New Orleans/popular)**

1. _____ team (coed/volleyball)

2. _____ subway (New York/hectic)

3. _____ rental (movie/X-rated)

4. _____ freeway (congested/endless)

5. _____ program (educational/worthwhile)

6. _____ encyclopedia (multivolume/valuable)

7. _____ question (surprising/trick)

8. _____ park (amusement/deserted/large)

9. _____ cloth (batik/orange/unusual)

10. _____ novel (new/Spanish/well-received)

56.1 Using the present, the present perfect, and the past forms of verbs

Rewrite the following passage, adapted from "In a Jumbled Drawer" by Stephen Jay Gould, by adding appropriate forms of *have* and main-verb endings or forms for the italicized verbs in parentheses. (See *The Everyday Writer*, pp. 396–401.)

As my son _____ (*grow*), I _____ (*monitor*) the

changing fashions in kiddie culture for words expressing deep admiration—

what I _____ (*call*) "cool" in my day, and my father

_____ (*designate*) "swell." The half-life _____ (*seem*) to be

about six months, as "excellent" (with curious lingering emphasis on the

first syllable) _____ (*give*) way to "bad" (extended, like a sheep bleat, long enough to turn into its opposite), to "wicked," to "rad" (short for

radical). The latest incumbent—"awesome"— _____ (*possess*) more

staying power, and _____ (*reign*) for at least two years.

56.2 Using specified forms of verbs

Using the subjects and verbs provided, write the specified sentences.
(See *The Everyday Writer,* pp. 396–401.) Example:

> **subject:** *Bernie* **verb:** *touch*
>
> **sentence using a present form:** Bernie touches the soft fur.
>
> **sentence using the auxiliary verb** *had*: Bernie had touched a squid before.

1. subject: *I* verb: *discuss*

   sentence using a past form:

   sentence using an auxiliary verb + the present participle form:

2. subject: *they* verb: *decide*

   sentence using a present form:

   sentence using an auxiliary verb + the past participle form:

3. subject: *geese* verb: *migrate*

   sentence using a past form:

   sentence using an auxiliary verb + the present participle form:

4. subject: *we* verb: *ask*

   sentence using a present form:

   sentence using the auxiliary *had* + the past participle form:

5. subject: *teen-agers* verb: *consume*

   sentence using a past form:

   sentence using the auxiliary verb *were* + the present participle form:

6. subject: *snakes* verb: *slither*

   sentence using a present form:

   sentence using an auxiliary verb + past participle form:

7. subject: *pasta* verb: *steam*

   sentence using a past form:

   sentence using an auxiliary verb + present participle form:

8. subject: *Yankees* verb: *win*

   sentence using a past form:

   sentence using an auxiliary verb + a present participle form:

9. subject: *hamburger* verb: *taste*

   sentence using a present form:

   sentence using an auxiliary verb + a past participle form:

10. subject: *pilots* verb: *fly*

    sentence using a past form:

    sentence using an auxiliary verb + a present participle form:

56.3 Identifying tenses and forms of verbs

From the following list, identify the form of each verb or verb phrase in each of the numbered sentences. (See *The Everyday Writer,* pp. 396–401.)

simple present	past perfect
simple past	present progressive
present perfect	past progressive

Example:

> **Judge Cohen considered the two arguments.** Simple past

1. She had forgotten the assignment.

2. This morning in class he is explaining his project.

3. My mother has driven the same Mazda for ten years.

4. Paul required special medical attention for years.

5. I have attempted that math problem several times now.

6. Just as we took our seats, the movie began.

7. As guests were arriving, Cheryl was still getting dressed.

8. She is exercising to reduce stress.

9. The elephant's floppy ears were delighting my son.

10. The twins Aimee and Sarah befuddle their teachers.

56.4 Using verbs appropriately

Each of the following sentences contains an error with verbs. Revise each sentence. (See *The Everyday Writer*, pp. 396–403.) Example:

Linguists ~~cannot~~ interpret hieroglyphics before they discovered the
Rosetta Stone.

could not

1. The Rosetta Stone was cover with inscriptions in two ancient languages, Greek and Egyptian.

2. Ancient Egyptian writing called hieroglyphics.

3. In the eighteenth century, no one can read hieroglyphics.

4. Very soon after its discovery, the French have made copies of the stone.

5. They sent these copies to scholars who were interesting in hieroglyphics.

6. By comparing the Egyptian writing with the Greek writing, the scholars interpreting the former.

7. The scholars were praise for their work.

8. They have carried out their work almost two hundred years ago.

9. Museum goers visit the stone for more than a hundred years.

10. We have visited it in 1966.

57.1 Using prepositions idiomatically

Insert one or more appropriate prepositions in each of the following sentences. (See *The Everyday Writer,* pp. 404–406.) Example:

We will have the answer _____ by _____ four o'clock this afternoon.

1. Newspapers and magazines report problems _____ elementary education.

2. Some articles say that teachers give attention only _____ children who are disruptive.

3. Other articles report on schools _____ areas of poverty and crime.

4. These articles say schools can't solve problems _____ themselves.

5. How can schools help when children arrive _____ the morning without breakfast?

6. Education needs participation _____ all of us.

7. Classrooms need books _____ their shelves.

8. Children should fall _____ love with reading.

9. Children should have pencils _____ their pencil cases.

10. They should get to school precisely _____ time.

57.2 Recognizing and using two-word verbs

Identify each italicized expression as either a two-word verb or as a verb + preposition. (See *The Everyday Writer*, pp. 406–407.) Example:

Look up John Brown the next time you're in town. two-word verb

1. Shortly after the French invasion of Egypt, the British *struck at* Napoleon.

2. By 1801, the French forces in Egypt were compelled to *fall back*.

3. The French *gave up* the Rosetta Stone reluctantly.

4. The British *took* it *back*.

5. The Rosetta Stone is now in the British Museum, where millions of visitors have *looked at* it.

6. The camp counselor *handed* the candy *out* as if it were gold.

7. *Put* the garbage *out* on the sidewalk, please.

8. Don't *put* yourself *out* on my behalf.

9. The frog *turned into* a prince.

10. The car *turned into* the driveway.

58.1 Expressing subjects and objects explicitly

Revise the following sentences or nonsentences so that they have explicit subjects and objects as necessary. If a sentence does not contain an error, write C. (See *The Everyday Writer*, pp. 407–408.) Example:

There is
Is a coffee bar in my apartment building.
^

1. Is of great importance that I know Yiddish, a dying language, according to some observers.

2. Snowed during my entire vacation.

3. No hot water tomorrow.

4. Having a great time; wish you were here.

5. We were losing patience with her because was always late.

6. There's no difference between us.

7. The poster publicizing the charity said, "Give!" in big letters.

8. We walked to the mailbox and mailed.

9. "I will now go to my chambers and consider," explained Judge Cohen.

10. Was even windier in Chicago than I'd expected.

58.2 Editing for English word order

Revise the following sentences as necessary. If a sentence does not contain an error, write C. (See *The Everyday Writer,* pp. 408–409.) Example:

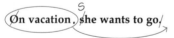

1. Chocolate eats the baby messily.

2. To sleep he wishes to go now.

3. "Speak fluently English," ordered the instructor.

4. John watches videos incessantly.

5. Desserts some restaurant guests would like to begin with.

6. She not can pronounce all English sounds.

7. A week's vacation he expects.

8. Put on the table the silverware.

9. Slow and easy wins the race.

10. Comes in first the runner from Kenya.

58.3 Using noun clauses, infinitives, and gerunds appropriately

Revise the following sentences as necessary so that each contains an appropriate noun clause, infinitive, or gerund positioned well. If a sentence does not contain an error, write C. (See *The Everyday Writer*, pp. 409–411.) Example:

>   *that*
> **It pleases me ^you like me.**

1. Makes me very proud that my English vocabulary is expanding.

2. It annoys the teacher we don't practice conversation.

3. What he has to say is of great interest to me.

4. Is important that we think in English.

5. I enjoy to study languages of native Americans.

6. I expect understanding more as I proceed with my studies.

7. We appreciated to get the invitation.

8. I agree to invest at least three hours a week in improving my English.

9. Her mother stopped to drive on her ninetieth birthday.

10. It is obvious that she made the right decision.

58.4   Using adjective clauses well

Revise the following sentences so that each includes an appropriate adjective clause positioned well. Make sure the sentence does not include unnecessary words or omit necessary relative pronouns. If a sentence does not contain an error, write C. (See *The Everyday Writer,* pp. 411–413.) Example:

The doctor prescribed medicine for her headache. that was no help.

1. Who has red hair the young man is picking up English very quickly.

2. The textbook that I am using it contains many examples of English sentences.

3. The class in that I enrolled has only a few students.

4. The class dinner we cooked together represented food from a dozen countries.

5. The chef works at my club helped by lending us pots and pans.

6. A reporter attended the dinner and wrote an article which he praised the chefs in it.

7. The results of the test, which we all prepared for, demonstrate the progress that we have made.

8. I want that is the newest the textbook.

9. The book that is the biggest is not necessarily the best.

10. The student practices the most gains the most.

58.5 Writing conditional sentences

Revise each of the following sentences so that both the *if*-clause and the main, or independent, clause contain appropriate verb forms. If a sentence does not contain an error, write *C*. (See *The Everyday Writer*, pp. 413–414.) Example:

                                  have stayed
  If you had loved me, I would ~~stay~~.

1. If the Rosetta Stone was not discovered, it would have been much more difficult to decipher hieroglyphics.

2. If I win a fellowship, I would go to graduate school.

3. If you had read the instructions, you had been finished assembling the desk by now.

4. If John Kennedy were alive today, he would question what we see as progress.

5. If he did not wear a seat belt, he would not have survived.

6. When you feel the flu coming on, you should consider getting more rest.

7. She will face months of therapy if the tests were positive.

8. If I'd known you were coming, I would bake a cake.

9. When she is good, she is very good, but when she is bad, she is horrid.

10. If it stopped raining, we will go biking.

Answers to the Even-Numbered Exercises

FREQUENTLY ASKED QUESTIONS

EXERCISE 3.1 Recognizing and eliminating the twenty most common errors

2. [Errors are in the second, third, and fourth sentences.] Setting up entails claiming your own territory, which you do by laying out your oversized beach towel and by turning your radio on loud enough to mark your domain without disturbing anyone else. This action should help you blend in with the locals.

4. [The error is in the first sentence.] Assateague is perfect for those who want to simply lie out in the sun, go swimming, and walk along the coast.

6. [The errors are in the third sentence.] Nothing fit my mood, and as my clothes fell on my bed, not one thing caught my eye.

8. Chips and sauces are not the only thing you get free refills on; you also get free refills on all nonalcoholic beverages, such as soda and tea. The servers are very good about getting you more of both things when you need refills. Usually you do not even have to ask.

10. [The errors are in the third sentence.] And if you get extremely lost, pulling off and asking will be the easiest way to get on track.

12. As I dribbled around the center, he stopped the defensive player not by using his hands but by using his big body.

14. [The error is in the second sentence.] They try to get the person's attention but never do what they planned to do.

16. [The error is in the first sentence.] On the other hand, what if you don't care for your partner—or even worse—your partner doesn't care for you?

18. [The error is in the last sentence.] "Come on. The bell rang. Class is over."

20. [The error is in the third sentence.] All the things that you do before, during, and after the party determine its success.

SENTENCE STYLE

EXERCISE 9.1 Matching subjects and predicates

SUGGESTED ANSWERS

2. To determine your rank, consult your supervisor.

   Ordinarily, your supervisor will advise you about your rank.

4. By not prosecuting white-collar crime as vigorously as we prosecute violent crime, we encourage white-collar criminals to ignore the law.

   We must prosecute white-collar crime as vigorously as violent crime unless we want to encourage white-collar criminals to ignore the law.

6. A stroke is a condition in which sufficient blood does not reach the brain.

   A stroke indicates a shortage of blood going to the brain.

8. Oedipus experiences the "shock of recognition" when he suddenly realizes that he has killed his father and married his mother.

   The "shock of recognition" comes when Oedipus suddenly realizes that he has killed his father and married his mother.

10. Europeans discovered Australia, but the British made it into a penal colony.

    Although it was a European discovery, Australia became a British penal colony.

EXERCISE 9.2 Making comparisons complete, consistent, and clear

SUGGESTED ANSWERS

2. Argentina and Peru were colonized by Spain, and Brazil was colonized by Portugal.

4. Was the dictatorship in Iraq any worse than dictatorships in many other countries?

6. Tim decided to take a nap, Michael to study for his chemistry test, and Susan to take a book back to the library.

8. Cats eat fish and liver, but they rarely eat steak.

10. As time went on, the baby became less animated and less interested.

EXERCISE 10.2 Writing sentences with subordination

SUGGESTED ANSWERS

2. When ticket sales were advertised for Barbra Streisand's first concert tour in years, fans lined up as many as forty-eight hours in advance.

4. *Working,* an important book by Studs Terkel, examines the situation of the American worker.

EXERCISE 11.1 Creating parallel words or phrases

SUGGESTED ANSWERS

2. My favorite pastimes include reading, exercising, and talking with friends.
4. I want not only hot fudge but also whipped cream.
6. Playing bridge, going for walks, and being alone together are activities that my grandparents enjoy.
8. I told my younger sister to keep out of my clothes and to keep away from my friends.
10. My motto is live, laugh, and enjoy.

EXERCISE 11.2 Revising sentences for parallelism

SUGGESTED ANSWERS

2. I will always remember how the girls dressed in green plaid skirts and the boys wore green plaid ties.
4. Needing a new pair of shoes and not being able to afford a pair is sad.
6. Too many students come to college to have fun, to find a husband or wife, or to put off having to go to work.
8. Her job was to show new products, to help with sales, and to participate in advertising.
10. Stress can result in low self-esteem, total frustration, sleeplessness, nervousness, or eventually suicide.

EXERCISE 12.1 Revising for verb tense and mood

SUGGESTED ANSWERS

2. Then, suddenly, the big day *arrived.* The children were still a bit sleepy, for their anticipation had kept them awake.
4. I think it better that Grandfather die painlessly, bravely, and with dignity than that he *continue* to live in terrible pain.
6. A cloud of snow powder rose as skis and poles *flew* in every direction.
8. The coroner asked that we be quiet and *attentive.*
10. Say no to drugs, and *consider* alcohol a drug, too!

EXERCISE 12.2 Eliminating shifts in voice and point of view

SUGGESTED ANSWERS

2. *Lionel gathered* the roses, and then he arranged them.

4. If *you* visit the local art museum, you will find on display recent prints by Greg Pfarr.

6. The first thing *we see* as we start down the slope is a green banner.

8. Sea anemones thrive in coastal tide pools, but *they* cannot survive outside the water for very long.

10. Tourists should be aware that road crews are busy on Highway 34, and *drivers* should expect some delay at the Oglesby Bridge construction site.

EXERCISE 12.3 Eliminating shifts between direct and indirect discourse

SUGGESTED ANSWERS

2. According to the article, the ozone layer is rapidly dwindling, *and the deterioration is endangering the lives of future generations.*

4. Oscar Wilde writes that books cannot be divided into moral and immoral categories *and that books are either written well or badly.*

EXERCISE 12.4 Eliminating shifts in tone and diction

SUGGESTED ANSWERS

2. George Washington was a leader of men; he was able to lead his army across the Potomac and into numerous battles with the British.

4. This land, which belongs to me, contains rare species of plants, and I cannot permit you to drive across it so carelessly.

EXERCISE 13.1 Emphasizing main ideas

SUGGESTED ANSWERS

2. Coast Guard personnel conduct boating safety classes, monitor emergency radio channels, and sometimes must risk their own lives to save others.

4. After distinguished service as a PT boat commander during World War II and after being elected to Congress, John Kennedy became president.

6. Al Unser blew a tire out, but thanks to his trusty pit crew and his ability to control the car in a tailspin, he sped across the finish line first.

8. Because of the bizarre nature of the clues and the fact that no one ever heard a thing, the case baffled inspectors. Eventually, however, they found the killer.

10. Margaret spent three years deciding whether medicine was right for her; then she was in medical school for over six years. She finally graduated last month.

EXERCISE 14.1 Eliminating unnecessary words and phrases

SUGGESTED ANSWERS

2. Many people tend to expand their sentences by adding unnecessary words.

4. I put on ten pounds shortly after I stopped exercising.

6. Today, welfare reform remains an important issue.

8. Aaron asked me to turn in his paper for him if he did not return to campus by 9 A.M.

10. We agree that the paper originally due on Monday will now be due on the following Friday.

SENTENCE GRAMMAR

EXERCISE 16.1 Identifying subjects and predicates

The subject is set in italics; the predicate is set in boldface.

2. *He* **was an army doctor, with a gray toothbrush moustache and a gruff voice.**

4. *The dog* **answered the sound with a whine.**

6. *All this* **was perplexing and upsetting.**

8. *I* **had halted on the road.**

10. *His mouth* **slobbered.**

EXERCISE 16.2 Identifying verbs and verb phrases

2. had been leaking

4. can collect; might run; should finish

6.　announced
8.　will include
10.　must submit

EXERCISE 16.3　Identifying nouns and articles

Nouns are set in italics; articles are set in boldface.

2.　*plagiarism*
4.　*Henderson's story;* **a;** *tale; theft; violation*
6.　**the;** *clock;* **the;** *wall*
8.　*Alice; secret*
10.　*broccoli; asparagus*

EXERCISE 16.4　Identifying pronouns and antecedents

Pronouns are set in italics; antecedents are set in boldface.

2.　**crowd;** *that; one; I*
4.　*They; themselves*
6.　*That;* **cup;** *which; you; mine*
8.　*Everybody; who*
10.　**senator;** *herself; her*

EXERCISE 16.5　Identifying adjectives and adverbs

Adjectives are set in italics; adverbs are set in boldface.

2.　**hilariously;** *the; sly; the; the; first*
4.　**unhappily;** *the; sleek; new; its*
6.　*The;* **most;** *instructive; the;* **unfortunately;** *the; longest*
8.　**Late;** *the; the;* **precipitously**
10.　**seriously; how; well;** *their; intense; public*

EXERCISE 16.6　Adding adjectives and adverbs

SUGGESTED ANSWERS

2.　The beautiful, athletic heroine marries the charming, bookish prince.

4. The tall, white candles gleamed brightly on the well-scrubbed tabletop.

6. Nobody saw the reportedly cute bear, but the forest ranger said it was unquestionably dangerous.

8. Our final chemistry assignment is due next Wednesday.

10. Her reticent employers nevertheless loudly praised her unstinting work for the famous Environmental Protection Agency.

EXERCISE 16.7   Identifying prepositions

2. around; across; into

4. During; down; between

6. according to; on

8. For; of

10. In

EXERCISE 16.8   Identifying conjunctions

2. nevertheless; as

4. but

6. not only . . . but also [two parts of a correlative conjunction]

8. until

10. neither . . . nor [two parts of a correlative conjunction]; therefore

EXERCISE 16.9   Identifying conjunctions and interjections

2. either . . . or (CORREL)

4. and (COORD); and (COORD); and (COORD); and (COORD); and (COORD)

6. so (COORD)

8. but (COORD)

10. Until (SUBORD)

EXERCISE 16.10   Identifying the parts of speech

2. Nike – noun (proper); want – verb; fitness – noun

4. relief – noun; can purchase – verb; the – article (adjective)

6. In – preposition; that – pronoun (relative); consistently – adverb

8. need – verb; truck – noun; like – preposition

10. really – adverb; actual – adjective; live – verb

EXERCISE 16.11 Identifying subjects

Complete subjects are set in italics; simple subjects are set in boldface.

2. *the new* **elevator**
4. *The long, low, intricately carved* **table**
6. *Rap* **music**
8. *Television talk* **shows**
10. *no* **time** *to study*

EXERCISE 16.12 Identifying predicates

Predicates are set in italics.

2. *made us a nation:* trans – made; do – us; oc – nation
4. *will never die:* intrans – will . . . die
6. *give Louise a toothache:* trans – give; io – Louise; do – a toothache
8. *tickled Lester under his arms:* trans – tickled; do – Lester
10. *made everyone melancholy:* trans – made; do – everyone; oc – melancholy

EXERCISE 16.13 Identifying prepositional phrases

2. in his vocabulary
4. out of the dugout

EXERCISE 16.14 Using prepositional phrases

SUGGESTED ANSWERS

2. Without fear, Socrates faced death.
4. Except for a few of his followers, everyone thought Socrates was crazy.
6. The treatment Socrates received appalled some contemporaries, Plato among them.
8. Socrates was Plato's teacher of philosophy.
10. Plato wrote the *Republic* in the form of a dialogue.

EXERCISE 16.15 Identifying verbal phrases

2. gerund – careful saving
4. part – Raised in Idaho; part – exploring nature

6. part – Feeling ill; inf – to cancel his date
8. gerund – Swimming every other morning; verbal is subject
10. part – ringing loudly; part – aching mightily

EXERCISE 16.16 Identifying prepositional, verbal, absolute, and appositive phrases

2. verbal – To listen to Patsy Cline; prep – to Patsy Cline
4. verbal – Floating on my back; prep – on my back
6. app – a sensitive child; prep – with a mixture; prep – of awe and excitement
8. verbal – Basking in the sunlight; prep – in the sunlight; prep – in reminiscence; prep – of birch trees
10. prep – of recreation; part – taking a nap

EXERCISE 16.17 Adding prepositional, verbal, absolute, and appositive phrases

SUGGESTED ANSWERS

2. After soaking up the sun and eating good food, she looked healthy when he saw her the second time.
4. The Sunday afternoon dragged to an absolute halt.
6. In addition to kissing babies, posing for pictures, and eating fried chicken, the candidates shook hands with the voters.
8. A late bloomer, Ben often thought regretfully about the past.
10. A young couple and their children, they lived in a trailer, crowded together like sardines.

EXERCISE 16.18 Using verbal, absolute, and appositive phrases to combine sentences

SUGGESTED ANSWERS

2. Our passports grasped in our hands, we waited to go through customs.
4. Relying too much on his computer was his downfall.
6. The large American cockroach, also known as the Palmetto bug and the water bug, likes moist environments.
8. Concentrating intensely on his experiments, he blocks out the rest of the world.
10. They both need to use the computer, a laptop.

EXERCISE 16.19 Identifying dependent clauses

Dependent clauses are set in italics.

2. *As a potential customer entered the store;* sub conj – As
4. *When she was deemed old enough to understand;* sub conj – when; *that her father had left home, not died;* rel pron – that
6. *which was Lynn's favorite;* rel pron – which
8. *than I had remembered;* sub conj – than
10. *that he was extremely tired;* rel pron – that

EXERCISE 16.20 Adding dependent clauses

SUGGESTED ANSWERS

2. The German government dismantled the Berlin wall, which had become a symbol of oppression.
4. Rob, who was a collector of jazz records, always borrowed money from friends.
6. We stood outside for an hour while the opening band played.
8. Because she was willing to stay home on weekends and study, Erin won the translation contest.
10. A man, whose memorial plaque hangs in the lobby, was killed in that mill in 1867.

EXERCISE 16.21 Distinguishing between phrases and clauses

Dependent clauses are set in italics; phrases are set in boldface.

2. **in our bare skins** – prep phrase
4. **in a zoo** – prep phrase; **for some animals and birds** – prep phrase
6. **to read Thoreau** – verbal phrase; **to enjoy him** – verbal phrase
8. (Note that *sets out,* here, is a two–word verb, not a verb + preposition.) **to develop a style** – verbal phrase; *when you read the words*
10. **of Charlotte's descendants** – prep phrase; **in the barn** - prep phrase; *when the warm days of spring arrive;* **of spring** - prep phrase; **of tiny spiders** – prep phrase; **emerging into the world** – verbal phrase; *into the world* – prep phrase

EXERCISE 16.22   Classifying sentences grammatically and functionally

2. complex, declarative
4. simple, declarative
6. simple, imperative

8. compound-complex, declarative
10. complex, interrogative

EXERCISE 17.1   Using irregular verb forms

2. made; found
4. lost; look
6. chose; become

8. thrown; been
10. fallen; broken; done

EXERCISE 17.2   Editing verb forms

2. sang—sung; begun—began
4. went—gone
6. brung—brought

8. rode—ridden
10. drank—drunk

EXERCISE 17.3   Distinguishing between *lie* and *lay, sit* and *set, rise* and *raise*

2. laid
4. lying
6. sat

8. raise
10. rose

EXERCISE 17.4   Deciding on verb tenses

2. have predicted/have been predicting
4. has arrived/arrives
6. rode/was riding
8. will have watched
10. rises

EXERCISE 17.5   Sequencing tenses

2. *Having left* England in December, the settlers *arrived* in Virginia in May.

4. *Having cut off* all contact with family, he *did* not *know* whom to ask for help.

6. Mitch Williams *threw* a curve even though the catcher *signaled/had signaled* a fast ball.

8. The news *had* just *begun* when our power *went out*. [Accept "*went out.*"]

10. *Will* you *tell* Grandpa about your wedding plans when he *visits* us in the summer?

EXERCISE 17.6 Converting the voice of a sentence

Answers may vary slightly.

2. Such things as elevators, subways, and closets *were avoided* by Marianne.

4. The first snow of winter *covered* the lawns and rooftops.

6. The next section of this report *analyzes* the experimental data.

8. Jerry *ate* the last doughnut in the box just a few minutes ago.

10. *Have* you *been told* about our house rules by Moira?

EXERCISE 17.7 Using subjunctive mood

2. was—were
4. was—were
6. correct
8. makes—make
10. contributes—contribute

EXERCISE 18.1 Selecting verbs that agree with their subjects

2. presents
4. supplies
6. is
8. holds
10. leaves

EXERCISE 18.2 Making subjects and verbs agree

2. Correct; *talking and getting up* is considered a single unit.
4. Correct
6. display—displays
8. Correct
10. intimidates—intimidate

12. Correct
14. was (second verb)—were

EXERCISE 19.1 Using adjectives and adverbs appropriately

2. negative—negatively; modifies *acts*
4. real—really; modifies *cold*; heavy—heavily; modifies *raining*
6. bad—badly; modifies *hurt*
8. well—good; modifies *instructor*
10. strict—strictly; modifies *brought up*; accept "modifies *brought*"

EXERCISE 19.2 Using comparative and superlative modifiers appropriately

SUGGESTED ANSWERS

2. more gentler—gentler *or* more gentle
4. to live longer—to live longer than men
6. the most priceless—priceless
8. lower—lowest
10. successfuler—more successful

EXERCISE 20.1 Revising sentences with misplaced modifiers

SUGGESTED ANSWERS

2. The city spent almost two million dollars on the new stadium that opened last year.
4. The clothes that I was giving away were full of holes.
6. Doctors recommend a new, painless test for cancer.
8. Before I decided to buy the stock, I knew that the investment would pay off dramatically.
10. The maintenance worker shut down the turbine that was revolving out of control.

EXERCISE 20.2 Revising squinting modifiers, disruptive modifiers, and split infinitives

SUGGESTED ANSWERS

2. The mayor promised that after her reelection she would not raise taxes.

After her reelection, the mayor promised that she would not raise taxes.

4. Doctors can now restore limbs that have been partially severed to functioning condition.

   Doctors can now restore limbs that have been severed to a partially functioning condition.

6. Eastern North America was covered in forest when Europeans arrived.

   When Europeans arrived, eastern North America was covered in forest.

8. The architect wanted to responsibly design public buildings eventually.

   The architect wanted eventually to design public buildings responsibly.

10. Because of the sudden trading, the stock exchange became a chaotic circus.

    The stock exchange became a chaotic circus because of the sudden trading.

12. After eating two chicken breasts, a baked potato, a tossed salad, and strawberry shortcake, Rico felt full.

    Rico felt full after eating two chicken breasts, a baked potato, a tossed salad, and strawberry shortcake.

14. She sang a selection of traditional folk songs and ballads in her first public concert.

    In her first public concert, she sang a selection of traditional folk songs and ballads.

EXERCISE 20.3   Revising dangling modifiers

SUGGESTED ANSWERS

2. When interviewing grieving relatives, reporters show no consideration for their privacy.

4. Chosen for their looks, newscasters often have weak journalistic credentials.

6. However unhappy I am with my part-time job, I have to put up with it.

8. When waiters are faced with a busy restaurant full of hungry people, their jobs can become very stressful.

10. No matter how costly a college education may be, my family insists on it.

12. Dressed and ready for the dance, she found that her car wouldn't start.

14. While cycling through southern France, I was impressed by the Roman ruins.

EXERCISE 21.1 Using subjective case pronouns

2.	they	8.	we
4.	We	10.	he
6.	she		

EXERCISE 21.2 Using objective case pronouns

2. Correct
4. Which of these books is for <u>me</u>?
6. We need two volunteers: <u>you</u> and Tom.
8. Correct
10. Correct

EXERCISE 21.3 Using possessive case pronouns

2. hers
4. his
6. mine (Accept any possessive pronoun in the noun form.)
8. its
10. Whose

EXERCISE 21.4 Using *who, whoever, whom,* or *whomever*

2.	Whoever	8.	whoever
4.	whom	10.	Whomever
6.	whoever		

EXERCISE 21.5 Using pronouns in compound structures, appositives, elliptical clauses; choosing between *we* and *us* before a noun

2.	he	10.	him
4.	he	12.	me
6.	she	14.	us
8.	us		

EXERCISE 21.6   Maintaining pronoun-antecedent agreement

SUGGESTED ANSWERS

2. Roommates do not always get along, but they can usually manage to tolerate each other temporarily.

4. Either Jack or Jill is always falling down hills.

6. Every house and apartment has its advantages and its drawbacks.

8. Correct

10. I often turn on the fan and the light and neglect to turn them off.

EXERCISE 21.7   Clarifying pronoun reference

SUGGESTED ANSWERS

2. Lear divides his kingdom between the two older daughters, Goneril and Regan, whose extravagant professions of love are more flattering than the simple affection of the youngest daughter, Cordelia. The consequences of this error in judgment soon become apparent, as the older daughters prove neither grateful nor kind to him.

4. New England helped to shape many aspects of American culture, including education, religion, and government. As New Englanders moved west, they carried their institutions with them.

6. Bill smilingly announced Ed's promotion to Ed.

   Bill smilingly announced his own promotion to Ed.

8. When drug therapy is combined with psychotherapy, the patients relate better and are more responsive to their therapists, and they are less vulnerable to what disturbs them.

10. Quint trusted Smith because Smith had worked for her before.

    Quint trusted Smith because she had worked for Smith before.

EXERCISE 22.1   Revising comma splices and fused sentences

Only one suggested answer is given for each numbered item.

2. Reporters today have no choice but to use computers.

4. My mother taught me to read, but my grandmother taught me to *love* to read.

6. Lincoln called for troops to fight the Confederacy; as a result, four more southern states seceded.

8. E. B. White died in 1985; his work nevertheless continues to inspire readers.

10. As the music lifted her spirits, she stopped sighing and began to sing.

12. One month she can't talk or even sit up by herself; the next she's standing wobbly-legged against the furniture and calling, "Ma, Ma."

14. The college of education receives applications from more individuals than it can admit, but the college carefully screens them all.

16. Perhaps this whole thing is a joke; then again, maybe it isn't.

18. The concert was sold out, so the promoters added another show.

20. When our diplomatic efforts failed, we prepared for war.

EXERCISE 23.1 Eliminating sentence fragments

SUGGESTED ANSWERS

2. Many Americans yearn to live with gusto.

4. The climbers had two choices: to go over a four-hundred-foot cliff or to turn back. They decided to make the attempt.

6. The president promoted one tax change: a reduction in the capital gains tax.

8. Offering good pay and the best equipment money can buy, organized crime has been able to attract graduates just as big business has.

10. Wollstonecraft believed in universal public education and in education that forms the heart and strengthens the body.

WORDS/GLOSSARY

EXERCISE 24.1 Using formal register

SUGGESTED ANSWERS

2. All candidates strive for the same results: to discredit their opponents and to persuade the majority of voters that they are qualified for the position.

4. The angrier she became over his actions, the more he rebelled and continued doing what he pleased.

6. Moby Dick's enormous size was matched only by Ahab's obsessive desire to destroy him.

8. This essay will refute Mr. Buckley's argument.

10. James Agee's most famous novel, *A Death in the Family*, focuses on a young boy and on what happens after his father is killed in an automobile accident.

EXERCISE 24.2 Checking for correct denotation

2. imminent/Correct word: eminent
4. purport/Correct word: report
6. Correct
8. illusion/Correct word: allusion
10. affective/Correct word: effective

EXERCISE 24.3 Revising sentences to change connotations

2. keep screaming

   Rewrite: Prochoice sympathizers consistently assert that a ban on abortion would drive abortion out of hospitals and into back alleys.

4. keep whining/bums/crazies/lazy

   Rewrite: Liberals consistently focus attention on the homeless, the mentally ill, and the unemployed.

6. packs/swarm/itching/finger/figurehead

   Rewrite: Each election year, delegations of Republicans gather at a national convention, eager to nominate a candidate.

8. conspiring

   Rewrite: The Democrats are planning a new education bill.

EXERCISE 24.4 Considering connotation

SUGGESTED ANSWERS

2. *tragic:* distressing, alarming, disturbing; *consumes:* defeats, feeds on, erodes; *displays:* champions, thrives on, builds up, promotes; *drama:* excitement, tension, vitality

4. *girl:* young lady, miss

EXERCISE 24.5 Using specific and concrete words

SUGGESTED ANSWERS

2. Cooing, singing, twittering—the early morning beckoning of birds outside my window makes it a treat to get up.

4. The valet stepped cautiously yet excitedly toward my Jeep.

6. My next-door neighbor is a nuisance, poking and prying into my life, constantly watching me as I enter and leave my house, and complaining about the noise when I am having a good time.

8. The president's speech touched on many important topics, including new tenure programs for professors, renovations on the student center, and the appointment of a new trustee.

10. After she smiled knowingly, the president answered the question by saying cutbacks were only a last resort.

EXERCISE 24.6 Thinking about similes and metaphors

SUGGESTED ANSWERS

2. *deep and soft like water moving in a cavern* (simile): compares the sound of her voice to water in a cavern, helping the reader to imagine the sound

4. *like veils of trailing lace* (simile): captures the delicateness of the fog

6. *"the mule of the world"* (metaphor): makes vivid the mention of burdens later in the sentence

8. *was a produce section* (metaphor): communicates the plenitude and variety of the garden

10. *A whip cracking in the wind* (metaphor): helps us not only see the flag but also hear it

EXERCISE 25.1 Identifying stereotypes

2. *old folks:* Assumes everyone in a nursing home is old, which is not necessarily the case. The tone is condescending, too.

4. *college kids:* Assumes all college students are eighteen to twenty-two years old, and assumes that all experience up to this time isn't "real-world." In fact, many college students have returned to school after years in the work force.

6. *irresponsible:* Overlooks the young people who manage not only to do well in school but also to participate in good causes and to be responsible toward their friends and family.

8. *Harvard-educated; belly-aching:* Assumes that doctors are elite, whining individuals.

EXERCISE 25.3 Rewriting to eliminate offensive references

SUGGESTED ANSWERS

2. Our skylight was installed last week by a carpenter. (Also acceptable: any version that omits mention of the carpenter's sex.)

4. These days secretaries have to know their word-processing skills. (*Or* These days a secretary must know word-processing.)

6. Those who don't appreciate classical music probably don't listen to the classical music station.

8. Actor Denzel Washington appeared at a charity benefit last night.

10. Acting as a spokesperson, Cynthia McDowell vowed that all elementary schoolteachers in the district would take their turns on the picket line until the school board agreed to resume negotiations.

EXERCISE 27.1   Recognizing correct spellings

2. to; too
4. noticeable; until
6. believe; lose
8. affects; success; than; its
10. develop; truly; successful
12. where; and
14. businesses; dependent
16. experience; exercise
18. categories; final
20. occasion; whether; weather

EXERCISE 27.3   Spelling plurals

2. mothers-in-law	8. phenomena
4. babies	10. roses
6. radios	12. turkeys

EXERCISE 28.1   Selecting the appropriate word

2. a while	12. preceded
4. bad	14. than
6. between	16. quotation
8. farther	18. reason
10. whether	20. disinterested

EXERCISE 28.2   Editing inappropiate words

2. The artist created a new *effect* by dribbling paint on the canvas.
4. Correct

6. The principal *could have been* more encouraging when talking to the parents.

8. *Let* the child have a chance to figure out the puzzle on her own.

10. I was ready for the final exam. (Drop *good and*.)

12. *It's* never a waste of time to check each instance of *its* and *it's* to be sure you've used the right homonym.

14. She *immigrated* to New York in the 1920s.

16. A small *percentage* of the graduates weren't qualified for the entry-level positions.

18. The supervisor and the trainee speak to each other *every day*.

20. Correct

PUNCTUATION / MECHANICS

EXERCISE 29.1 Using a comma to set off introductory elements

2. Unfortunately,

4. If you follow the instructions,

6. Correct

8. To become an Olympic competitor,

10. Startled by the explosion,

EXERCISE 29.2 Using a comma in compound sentences

SUGGESTED ANSWERS

2. Joan Didion's nonfiction is renowned, *but* her novels are also worthwhile.

4. The playwright disliked arguing with directors, *so* she avoided rehearsals.

6. The sun shone, *and* the sky was a clear, deep blue.

8. The geography final had me worried, *so* I studied for two hours after lunch.

10. She could not keep her eyes open, *for* she had been up all night.

EXERCISE 29.3 Recognizing restrictive and nonrestrictive elements

2. The clause *who rescued her puppy* is restrictive because only the man who rescued the puppy won the gratitude. The winning of eternal

gratitude is restricted to the man who rescued the puppy. Therefore, the clause should not take commas.

4. The participial phrase *made of wood* is restrictive because the meaning of the sentence is not complete without it. That the houses are made of wood is what often allows them to survive earthquakes. Therefore, the phrase should not take commas.

6. The clause *who is fourteen years old* provides important information. Therefore, the clause should not take commas.

8. The clause *which bears a striking resemblance to my bedroom* provides important but extra information. Therefore, it should be set off with commas.

10. Do not set off the phrase *overlooking the ocean* with commas, or your readers won't know what kind of house costs $500,000.

12. The phrase that tells about the president's term is providing additional information but information that is not crucial to the rest of the sentence. Therefore, *elected for a six-year term* should be set off from the rest of the sentence.

14. *Birds' hearts have four chambers, whereas reptiles' have three.* The second clause is a whole new piece of information, which does not bear directly on the first clause. Use a comma to separate certain adverb clauses that occur at the end of a sentence.

EXERCISE 29.4   Using commas to set off items in a series

2. We bought zucchini, peppers, and tomatoes at the market.

4. The spider's orange body resembles a colored dot amidst eight long, black legs.

6. Superficial observation does not provide accurate insight into people's lives—how they feel, what they believe in, how they respond to others.

8. I timidly offered to help a loud, overbearing, lavishly dressed customer.

10. The moon circles the earth, the earth revolves around the sun, and the sun is just one star among many in the Milky Way galaxy.

EXERCISE 29.5   Using commas to set off parenthetical and transitional expressions, contrasting elements, interjections, direct address, and tag questions.

2. The West, in fact, has become solidly Republican in presidential elections.

4. Ladies and gentlemen, I bid you farewell.

6. Hey, stop ogling that construction worker!

8. "Bill, could you read over the third paragraph?"

10. Joey enjoys chocolate milkshakes, but only those made with vanilla ice cream.

EXERCISE 29.6 Using commas with dates, addresses, titles, numbers, and quotations

2. Ithaca, New York, has a population of about 30,000.

4. MLA headquarters are at 10 Astor Place, New York, New York 10003.

6. Correct

8. Correct

10. Correct

EXERCISE 29.7 Eliminating unnecessary and inappropriate commas

2. Observers watch facial expressions and gestures and interpret them.

4. Our supper that evening consisted of stale bologna sandwiches.

6. Sitting around the campfire, we felt boredom and disappointment.

8. The photographer Edward Curtis is known for his depiction of the West.

10. Driving a car and talking on the car phone at the same time demand care.

EXERCISE 30.1 Using semicolons to link clauses

2. City life offers many advantages; in many ways, however, life in a small town is much more pleasant.

4. Physical education forms an important part of a university's program; nevertheless, few students and professors clearly recognize its value.

6. Voltaire was concerned about the political implications of his skepticism; he warned his friends not to discuss atheism in front of the servants.

8. My high school was excessively competitive; virtually everyone went on to college, many to the top schools in the nation.

10. *Propaganda* is defined as the spread of ideas to further a cause; therefore, *propaganda* and *advertisement* are synonyms.

EXERCISE 30.2 Eliminating misused semicolons

2. If the North had followed up its victory at Gettysburg more vigorously, the Civil War might have ended sooner.

4. We must find a plan to provide decent health care, a necessity in today's life.

6. For four glorious but underpaid weeks, I'll be working in Yosemite this summer.

8. My current work-study job ends in two weeks. I'll need to find a new position starting next term.

10. Some gardeners want low-maintenance plants, limited grass to mow, and low water usage.

EXERCISE 31.1 Using periods appropriately

2. Cicero was murdered in 43 B.C.

4. She asked whether the operation had been founded by Jesse Jackson.

6. I just asked you what time it was. (*Or* I just asked you, "What time is it?")

8. Write the check to Richard Steins, M.D.

10. Please change the record. Then come sit down.

EXERCISE 31.2 Using question marks appropriately

2. Correct

4. Correct

6. Who said, "Give me liberty, or give me death"?

8. "Have you heard the one about the tourist and the barber?" he asked.

10. Learning how to be a curious traveler is a good way to find out about U.S. history.

EXERCISE 31.3 Using exclamation points appropriately

SUGGESTED ANSWERS

2. I screamed at Jamie, "You rat! You tricked me!"

4. Stop, thief!

6. What, exactly, do you want?

8. The only thing the surprised guest of honor could say was, "Well, I'll be!"

10. The child cried, "Ouch!" as her mother pulled off the bandage.

EXERCISE 32.1 Using apostrophes to signal possession

2. *Maria Callas's* opera performances are now the stuff of legend.

4. *Carol and Jim's* combined income dropped drastically after Jim lost his job.

6. Many smokers disregard the *surgeon general's* warnings.

8. The *governors'* attitudes changed after the convention.

10. *My friend's and my brother's* cars have the same kind of stereo system.

EXERCISE 32.2 Using apostrophes to create contractions

2. You've been listening to several folks as they've described how the United Way has helped them; now won't you please take out your checkbooks and help your neighbors?

4. Who'll the critics identify as the best new novelist of the decade?

6. For the test you'll be taking on Monday, you're required to have a pencil with No. 2 lead.

8. Who's responsible for that accident?

10. It's true that a snake can shed its own skin and can swallow much of its prey whole.

EXERCISE 33.1 Using quotation marks to signal direct quotations

2. "I'm going outside for some air," said Ryan, "but I'll only be a few minutes."

4. "I could not believe the condition of my hometown," he wrote.

6. Correct

8. Correct

10. To repeat their words, "The worst is behind us."

EXERCISE 33.2 Using quotation marks for definitions and titles

2. In Flannery O'Connor's short story "Revelation," colors symbolize passion, violence, sadness, and even God.

4. "The British," the guide told us, "knit sweaters for their teapots."

6. "Big Bill," a section of Dos Passos's book *U.S.A.,* opens with a birth.

8. The Beatles song "Love Me Do" catapulted the Beatles to international stardom.

10. In the episode "Driven to Extremes," *48 Hours* takes a humorous look at driving in New York City.

EXERCISE 33.3 Using quotation marks appropriately

SUGGESTED ANSWERS

2. What is Hawthorne telling the readers in "Rappaccini's Daughter"?

4. "Buddhist Economics" is not a chapter title you'll find in too many college textbooks.

6. One of Joyce Carol Oates's most shocking stories is "The Bingo Master"; in it, the triumph of brutality is devastating.

8. In his article "The Death of Broadway," Thomas M. Disch writes that "choreographers are, literally, a dying breed."[1]

10. One thought flashed through my mind as I finished *In Search of Our Mothers' Gardens:* "I want to read more of this writer's books." (This item without quotation marks around the second sentence is also acceptable.)

EXERCISE 34.1 Using parentheses and brackets

2. During my research, I found that a flat-rate income tax (a single-rate tax with no deductions) has its problems.

4. Many researchers used the Massachusetts Multiphasic Personal Inventory (MMPI) for hypnotizability studies.

6. That mantel clock (made in Germany in 1888) has been in the family since my father's grandmother brought it over with her in 1901.

8. The Republican party has not always been unsympathetic to feminist concerns (such as the Equal Rights Amendment [ERA], which the Nixon administration supported).

10. Then she turned and said, "Will you [meaning my father] be joining us for dinner?"

EXERCISE 34.2 Using dashes

2. Even if smoking is harmful—and there is no real proof of this assertion—it is unjust to outlaw smoking while other harmful substances remain legal.

4. Union Carbide's plant in Bhopal, India, sprang a leak—a leak that killed more than 2,000 people and injured an additional 200,000.

6. "I—wait—*no*—don't shoot—I'll tell you what you want to know."

8. We'll meet you for nine at Woodstock's for pizza—if Rob's aging Buick can get there.

10. Several kinds of lace—among them Alencon, Honiton, and Maltese—take their names from their place of origin.

EXERCISE 34.3   Using colons

2. Another example is taken from Psalm 139:16.

4. Shifting into German, Kennedy declared: "Ich bin ein Berliner."

6. Gandhi urged four rules: tell the truth even in business, adopt more sanitary habits, abolish caste and religious divisions, and learn English.

8. *Signs of Trouble and Erosion: A Report on Education in America* was submitted to Congress and the president in January 1984.

10. Two buses go to Denver: one at 9:38 A.M. and one at 2:55 P.M.

EXERCISE 34.5   Reviewing punctuation marks

2. Gina, who is my father's cousin, lives in Florence.

4. The poems of Wallace Stevens are difficult at first; however, upon further reading their greatness becomes evident.

6. Whereas Bartholomew kept calling the library a "bookhouse," I referred to it as "the house of naps."

8. When I read the judges' decision, I decided that they had not paid sufficient attention to the defense's arguments.

10. Correct

12. "I did not know that Ann was coming with us this evening," Peter said.

14. "Cold and windy," the weather report said.

16. Correct

18. *Where in the World Is Carmen Sandiego?*—an ever-popular and hard-to-stock game program—has just arrived on our shelves. (Accept parentheses in place of the dashes.)

20. Stock analysts refer to IBM (International Business Machines) as a blue-chip stock. (Accept quotation marks around *blue-chip stock*.)

EXERCISE 35.1   Capitalizing

2. We had a choice of fast-food, Chinese, or Italian restaurants.

4. The Council of Trent was convened to draw up the Catholic response to the Protestant Reformation.

6. I wondered if my new Levi's were faded enough.

8. I will cite the novels of Vladimir Nabokov, in particular *Pnin* and *Lolita*.

10. My favorite song by Cole Porter is "You'd Be So Nice to Come Home To."

EXERCISE 36.1 Using abbreviations

2. An MX missile, which is 71 feet long and 92 inches around, weighs 190,000 pounds.

4. In 1991, Representative William Gray became president of the United Negro College Fund.

6. Unfortunately, the five-cent candy bar is a relic of the past.

8. The local radio station has a broadcast range of seventy-five miles.

10. Dostoyevsky was influenced by many European writers—for example, Dickens, Stendhal, and Balzac.

EXERCISE 36.2 Spelling out numbers and using figures

SUGGESTED ANSWERS

2. Time will provide perspective on the economic crises of the eighties. (*Or* 1980s.)

4. The invasion of Kuwait began on August 2, 1990.

6. Cable TV is now available to 72 percent of the population.

8. In the thirty-five to forty-four age group, the risk is estimated to be about 1 in 2,500. (*Or* 35-to-44 age group; if you treat the three-word expression as a compound modifier, it would become unwieldy to include hyphenated numbers spelled out.)

10. The amulet measured 1 1/8 by 2 2/5 inches.

EXERCISE 37.1 Using italics

2. Is Samuel Beckett's play *Endgame* a sequel to Shakespeare's *King Lear*?

4. The word *veterinary* comes from the Latin *veterinarius.*

6. Flying the *Glamorous Glennis*, named for his wife, Chuck Yeager was the first pilot to fly faster than the speed of sound.

8. *The Waste Land* is a long and difficult but ultimately rewarding poem.

10. The White Star liner *Titanic* sank in the North Atlantic in 1912.

EXERCISE 38.1 Using hyphens in compounds and with prefixes

2. pre-World War II

4. Correct

6. self-important

8. thirty-three

10. a politician who is fast-talking (*Fast-talk* is commonly found in dictionaries; thus hyphenation is correct even though the compound adjective comes after the noun.)

EXERCISE 38.2 Using hyphens appropriately

2. The drumbeating and hand clapping signaled that the parade was near.

4. Suicide among teen-agers has tripled in the past thirty-five years.

6. Both pro- and anti-State Department groups registered complaints.

8. In Bizet's *Carmen*, the ill-fated Carmen is betrayed by her fickleness.

10. The beautifully written essay earned high praise.

FOR MULTILINGUAL WRITERS

EXERCISE 55.1 Identifying count and noncount nouns

In his book [**count**] Hiroshima, John Hersey tells the story [**count**] of six people [**count**] who survived the destruction [**noncount**] of Hiroshima on August 6, 1945. The bomb [**count**] detonated at 8:15 in the morning [**count**]. When the explosion [**count**] occurred, Mrs. Hatsuyo Nakamura was looking out her window [**count**] and watching a neighbor [**count**] at work [**noncount in this context**] on his house [**count**]. The force [**count**] of the explosion [**count**] lifted her into the air [**noncount**] and carried her into the next room [**count**], where she was buried by roofing tiles [**count**] and other debris [**noncount**]. When she crawled out, she heard her daughter [**count**], Myeko, calling out; she was buried up to her waist [**count**] and could not move.

EXERCISE 55.2 Using appropriate determiners; stating plural forms explicitly

2. Napoleon, the French ruler, invaded Egypt with *many* soldiers.

4. At Rosetta, near the Nile, some French soldiers were building *a* fort.

6. The stone contained three *sections* of writing.

8. The stone became the basis for *a* huge insight into ancient writing.

10. We do not know what future *digs* will uncover. (*or* a future dig)

EXERCISE 55.4   Positioning modifiers

2. hectic New York subway
4. endless congested freeway
6. valuable multivolume encyclopedia
8. large deserted amusement park
10. well-received new Spanish novel

EXERCISE 56.2   Using specified forms of verbs

SUGGESTED ANSWERS

2. They decide the defendant's fate with their verdict.
   They had decided the defendant's fate within an hour.
4. We ask only for a little of your time.
   We had asked for a meeting, but the dean turned us down.
6. Snakes slither on the ground near the campsite.
   Snakes had slithered on my grandmother's new carpet.
8. The Yankees won the play-offs.
   Are the Yankees winning?
10. Pilots flew aircraft as early as the 1920s.
    Pilots are flying greater distances these days.

EXERCISE 56.3   Identifying tenses and forms of verbs

2. present progressive
4. simple past
6. simple past; simple past
8. present progressive
10. simple present

EXERCISE 56.4   Using verbs appropriately

2. Ancient Egyptian writing *is* called [*was called*] hieroglyphics.
4. Very soon after its discovery, the French *made* copies of the stone.
6. By comparing the Egyptian writing with the Greek writing, the scholars *interpreted* the former.
8. They *carried* out their work almost two hundred years ago.
10. We *visited* it in 1966.

EXERCISE 57.1   Using prepositions idiomatically

2. to   8.   in
4. by   10. on
6. by/of

EXERCISE 57.2   Recognizing and using two-word verbs

2. two-word verb   8.   two-word verb
4. two-word verb   10. verb + preposition
6. two-word verb

EXERCISE 58.1   Expressing subjects and objects explicitly

SUGGESTED ANSWERS

2.   It snowed during my entire vacation.
4.   I'm having a great time; I wish you were here.
6.   Correct
8.   We walked to the mailbox and mailed the letter.
10. It was even windier in Chicago than I'd expected.

EXERCISE 58.2   Editing for English word order

SUGGESTED ANSWERS

2.   He wishes to go to sleep now.
4.   Correct
6.   She cannot pronounce all English sounds.
8.   Put the silverware on the table.
10. The runner from Kenya comes in first.

EXERCISE 58.3   Using noun clauses, infinitives, and gerunds appropriately

SUGGESTED ANSWERS

2.   It annoys the teacher that we don't practice conversation.
4.   It is important that we think in English.
6.   I expect to understand more as I proceed with my studies.

8. Correct
10. Correct

EXERCISE 58.4 Using adjective clauses well

SUGGESTED ANSWERS

2. The textbook that I am using contains many examples of English sentences.
4. Correct
6. A reporter attended the dinner and wrote an article in which he praised the chefs.
8. I want the textbook that is the newest.
10. The student who practices the most gains the most.

EXERCISE 58.5 Writing conditional sentences

SUGGESTED ANSWERS

2. If I win a fellowship, I will go to graduate school.
4. Correct
6. Correct
8. If I'd known you were coming, I would've baked a cake.
10. If it stops raining, we will go biking.